THE
STUDENT
VEGAN
COOKBOOK

TIL RACHEL ♡

Her kommer en forsinket julegave.
Takk for at inspirerer meg til å ta
bedre vare på verden.

Du er super!

Stor klem fra din favoritt
flatmate

julen 2021

Brimming with creative inspiration, how-to projects, and useful information to enrich your everyday life, Quarto Knows is a favorite destination for those pursuing their interests and passions. Visit our site and dig deeper with our books into your area of interest: Quarto Creates, Quarto Cooks, Quarto Homes, Quarto Lives, Quarto Drives, Quarto Explores, Quarto Gifts, or Quarto Kids.

First Published in 2021 by The Harvard Common Press, an imprint of The Quarto Group,
100 Cummings Center, Suite 265-D, Beverly, MA 01915, USA.
T (978) 282-9590 F (978) 283-2742 QuartoKnows.com

The Harvard Common Press titles are also available at discount for retail, wholesale, promotional, and bulk purchase. For details, contact the Special Sales Manager by email at specialsales@quarto.com or by mail at The Quarto Group, Attn: Special Sales Manager, 100 Cummings Center, Suite 265-D, Beverly, MA 01915, USA.

25 24 23 22 21   1 2 3 4 5

ISBN: 978-0-7603-7307-1

Digital edition published in 2021

Library of Congress Control Number: 2021937230

Design: Amy Sly
Photography: Hannah Kaminsky except pages 9, 12, 17, 21 are Shutterstock
Illustration: Shutterstock

Printed in China

THE STUDENT VEGAN COOKBOOK

85 Incredible Plant-Based Recipes That Are Cheap, Fast, Easy, and Super Healthy

Hannah Kaminsky

HARVARD
COMMON
PRESS

WHAT'S FOR DINNER?

NOM NOM NOM . . . .

DON'T FORGET THE SYRUP!

Contents

BEST RECIPE,

LETTUCE
CILANTRO
BELL PEPPERS
TOMATOES
AVOCADOS
CORN ON THE COB
VEGETABLE STOCK
YELLOW CORNMEAL

Introduction

Wobbling back from the four-mile journey to the health food co-op, arms loaded with overstuffed grocery bags, the trip back to the freshman residence halls could be a harrowing journey. Resources for fresh, affordable produce were far and few between, so if I didn't load up once a week, I'd be relegated to eating frozen spinach for dinner, microwaved with a splash of hot sauce, at best. Even with unlimited time and ingredients, I can't say I'd have known what to do with them.

Making the transition to campus life at an early age, I had no idea what to expect. How do you meet people and make friends out of 28,000 strangers? When is there time to fit in studies, clubs, parties, *and* sleep? Most importantly, though, what is there to *eat*?

Food worried me most of all, more than making the grade. As a fledgling vegan in an age when the concept was largely misunderstood, I was on my own in this strange land of restrictive meal plans and lackluster cafeteria food. I had to learn to cook, quickly, or disrupt lectures with the roar of my growling stomach. In the beginning, it was tubs of prepared hummus eaten with a spoon that got me through the day, for lack of any other easy options.

Mercifully, it's a completely different world out there for plant-based options. With the profusion of frozen meatless meals, healthier snacks, and even decadent desserts, you don't need to be an accomplished cook to eat well. The situation might be a bit different at school, however, since some institutions are still stuck in the past, with outdated facilities and government-subsidized menus. No matter the situation, there's never been a better opportunity to start cooking.

Feed yourself, win over dates, and impress your parents all with this one essential skill. If you learn nothing else during your student years, it would still be time well spent.

SHARING IS CARING

While you're unlikely to find a state-of-the-art kitchen with all the bells and whistles, many residence halls have a communal cooking space for everyone to share. That said, lower your expectations at least a few notches before you see the lay of the land, as it isn't always pleasant or convenient. Your fellow roommates (or apartment-mates) might not be so fastidious about cleaning, so brace yourself for piles of someone else's week-old dirty dishes in the sink, or worse. I recall a particular forlorn pumpkin stashed in the fridge during my freshman year that overstayed its welcome long after Halloween. Eventually, it became a science experiment to see just how moldy it could become before the stench became entirely overbearing and forced an evacuation of the building. I think the mark it left in the vegetable bin might still be there to this day.

The key to avoiding such distasteful frustrations is communication. Often, students who leave a mess in the kitchen don't mean to be rude—they're just too tired or busy to take care of the cleaning right away, and then promptly forget about such little details. We've all been there, right? When you're trying to snag a quick bite before rushing off to class some crusty old sauté pan is the least of your worries. Students don't realize that the cleaning staff isn't going to come in and clean up after them. Put up a sign in the kitchen as a gentle reminder, but more importantly, be direct and firm about ground rules.

In addition to cleaning, you can address issues like how much storage space each student can use and how to label your food so others know it's off-limits. This is especially important if you're saving up your hard-earned money on vegan specialty ingredients, only to have them "disappear" overnight. Even if you have shared fridge or freezer space, this is why I would still recommend splurging on a private mini fridge for your room. Maybe I have trust issues, but I couldn't risk seeing my precious staples get carelessly devoured by hungry hordes of sleep-deprived students.

Even if your communal kitchen is immaculate, that doesn't necessarily mean it's convenient to use for every meal. If you live on the fourth floor, it's a pain to go down to the basement in your pajamas, bleary-eyed and ravenous every morning, and begin crafting a full recipe from scratch. This is where batch cooking comes in! Many of these recipes are designed to make more than one serving, and that's not necessarily because you want to feed the whole residence hall. Some things, like soups and stews in particular, keep beautifully for a number of days, so you can simply heat and eat later on. It would be wise to pick up a set of reusable airtight containers to store leftovers; glass are my favorite option for durability, since you can place them directly in the microwave to reheat with ease. Always label your containers with the contents and date, so you don't wonder what the heck it is the next time you unearth your edible treasures.

Should your building lack even the most basic cooking equipment, don't panic. If you know friends or family in the area, plan cooking dates to visit and take advantage of their generosity. It's a good opportunity to catch up, take a break from your studies, and share the tasty results together, too.

PANTRY RAID

Whether it's found in a conventional kitchen cabinet or takes up residence in a storage container stuffed underneath the bed, your pantry is essential for eating well on a dime, anytime. Staples for every budget should include:

Canned beans Dried are more cost-effective, but there's no beating the convenience of popping open a can and cooking right away. You can find most varieties for a dollar or less, which makes them entirely affordable in any event.

Grains Rice, quinoa, barley, millet, amaranth—the sky is the limit for dried grains! Hit up your local health food store to scope out the bulk bins. You can mix and match grains, as long as they have similar cooking times.

Spices and herbs These are the keys to beating the blahs. You could cook the same basic recipe every single day, but season it differently, and never get bored. There's no shame in taking a shortcut with blends, such as Italian seasoning, Creole seasoning, curry powder, or pumpkin pie spice, to make it easier to hit that perfectly balanced flavor.

Carbs I'm talking about bread, pasta, tortillas, and the like. Seek out gluten-free varieties if needed. These are the foundation of the food pyramid for good reason: satisfying meals start with healthy, high-fiber carbohydrates for long-lasting energy.

Fats Olive oil, coconut oil, and vegan butter are the lubricants that prevent food from sticking mercilessly to skillets, make nutrients more bioavailable, and simply make food taste better. Just a little dab will do you, so there's no need to buy tons. Spend a little bit more on higher quality options, and that investment will go a long way.

Sweeteners Plain sugar is an easy answer when you need something sweet, but for more flavor, try agave or maple syrup. Don't overlook the world of alternative sweeteners, such as stevia or monk fruit. These zero-calorie options are especially useful for those who need to watch their blood sugar and are ideal for adding to beverages. Bear in mind that they do bake differently from conventional options, and can't be swapped out 1:1.

Shelf-stable vegetables and sauces Things like corn, diced tomato, and pumpkin puree are meals just waiting to happen. Don't forget about marinara sauce, which is good for so much more than just pasta. Consider it an instant soup starter for that classic tomato bisque!

Nuts and seeds These are great for snacking when you're on the go, or tossing into salads for a more satisfying bite. No pantry is complete without a nut butter, be it classic peanut, almond, or something more exotic. There's nothing wrong with a good old PB + J sandwich when you're just too tired to cook.

INGREDIENT GLOSSARY

Beyond the basics, here are some ingredients I call for in the following recipes that might bear further explanation.

Agave Nectar

Derived from the same plant as tequila but far less potent, this syrup is made from the condensed juice found at the core of the agave cactus. It is available in both light and dark varieties; the dark possesses a more nuanced, complex, and somewhat floral flavor, while the light tends to provide only a clean sweetness. Considered a less refined form of sugar, agave nectar has a much lower glycemic index than many traditional granulated sweeteners, and is therefore consumed by some diabetics in moderation.

All-Purpose Flour

While wonderful flours can be made from all sorts of grains, beans, nuts, and seeds, the gold standard in everyday baking and cooking is still traditional "all-purpose" wheat flour. Falling texturally somewhere in between cake flour and bread flour, it works as a seamless binder, strong foundation, and neutral base. It's an essential pantry staple for me, stocked in my cupboard at all times. All-purpose flour may be labeled in stores as unbleached white flour or simply "plain flour." Gluten-free all-purpose flour is also widely available now in mainstream markets and can be substituted at a 1:1 ratio for those sensitive to wheat.

Almond Meal/Flour

Almond flour is nothing more than raw almonds ground down into a fine powder, light and even in consistency, which makes it ideal for baking, while almond meal is generally a bit coarser. To make your own, just throw a pound or so of completely unadulterated almonds into your food processor, and pulse until floury. It's helpful to freeze the almonds in advance so that they don't overheat and turn into almond butter. You can also create a finer texture by passing the initial almond meal through a fine sieve to sift out the larger pieces. Due to their high oil content, ground nuts can go rancid fairly quickly. If you opt to stock up and save some for later, be sure to store the freshly ground almond flour in an airtight container in the refrigerator or freezer. To cut down on labor and save a little time, almond flour or meal can be purchased in bulk from natural food stores.

Aquafaba

It's the not-so-secret ingredient taking the world by storm, dubbed a "miracle" by some and a food science breakthrough by others. In case you're not already a fervent fan, aquafaba is the excess liquid found in any ordinary can of chickpeas. Technically, any bean can produce aquafaba, but the unique ratio of protein and starch in chickpeas has been found to best mimic the binding and whipping properties previously only seen in egg whites. Different brands will yield slightly different results, but I've never found any that are complete duds. For more delicate applications like meringues or marshmallow fluff, you can always concentrate your aquafaba to create a stronger foam matrix by cooking it gently on the stove and reducing some of the water.

Arrowroot Powder/Flour

Thanks to arrowroot, you can thicken sauces, puddings, and mousses with ease. This white powder is very similar to kudzu and is often compared to other starchy flours. However, arrowroot is so fine that it produces much smoother, creamier results, and is less likely to stick together and form large lumps. It also thickens liquids much more quickly than cornstarch or potato starch, without leaving an unpleasant, raw sort of cereal flavor behind.

Butter

It's a basic kitchen staple, but good dairy-free butter can be quite elusive if you don't know what to look for. Some name brands contain whey or other milk derivatives, while others conceal the elusive, animal-derived vitamin D3, so be alert when scanning ingredient labels. For ease, I prefer to use it in stick format. Never try to substitute spreadable butter from a tub! These varieties have much more water to allow them to spread while cold, and will thus bake and cook differently. I always use unsalted butter unless otherwise noted, but you are welcome to use salted as long as you remove about ¼ teaspoon of salt per ¼ cup of butter from the recipe. Overly salted food is one of the first flaws that diners notice, so take care with your seasoning and always adjust to taste.

Chia Seeds

Yes, this is the same stuff that makes chia pets so green and fuzzy, and yes, the seeds are edible! Tiny but mighty, these seeds are special because they form a gel when mixed with liquid. This makes them a powerful binder when trying to replace eggs or when flaxseeds are in short supply. Store in the freezer for a longer shelf life, and grind them before using in baked goods to maintain an even crumb texture.

Chickpea (Garbanzo Bean) Flour

Gaining in popularity as a versatile gluten-free flour, chickpea flour is just what you might imagine: nothing but dried, finely ground chickpeas. When used in baking, it can be used as a substitute for 20 to 25 percent of the wheat flour called for in a recipe or to add a toothsome density to cakes or cookies. It can also be cooked with water like polenta and eaten as a hot porridge, or let the mixture set overnight in a baking dish, slice, and then fry to make what is called chickpea panisse. Just be warned that eaten raw (if, say, someone decided to sample raw cookie batter that contains chickpea flour) it is very bitter and unpleasant.

Chickpea flour should be readily available in most grocery stores in the baking or natural foods section, but if you have a powerful blender with a dry grinding container, you can make your own from dried, split chickpeas (also known as chana dal). Process 2 cups of legumes at a time, and use the plunger to keep things moving. Once finely ground, let the dust settle for a few minutes before removing the lid of the container.

Chocolate

Chocolate is chocolate, right? Oh, if only it were so simple. Needless to say, conventional white and milk chocolate are out of the picture, but some so-called dark chocolates still don't make the dairy-free cut. Even those that claim to be "70% cacao solids, extra-special dark" may have milk solids or butterfat lurking within. Don't buy the hype or the fillers! Stay vigilant and check labels for milk-based ingredients, as unadulterated chocolate is far superior. Semisweet has approximately half as much sugar as cocoa solids, and bittersweet tends to have even less. Baker's chocolate is always vegan and entirely unsweetened, so it has intense chocolate flavor, but isn't the tastiest option for eating out of hand. Dark chocolate is somewhat of a catchall term that has no official or legal definition.

Coconut Milk

When I call for coconut milk in this book, I'm referring to regular, full-fat coconut milk. That fat is necessary for creating a smooth, creamy mouthfeel, and of course a richer taste. Light coconut milk or coconut milk beverages found in aseptic containers may be suitable in some cases for particularly calorie-conscious cooks, but such a substitution is likely to have detrimental effects on the overall texture of the dish. For best results, treat yourself

to the genuine article. Plain coconut milk is found canned in the ethnic foods aisle of the grocery store. You can make it yourself from fresh coconut meat, but in most cases, the added hassle honestly isn't worth the expense or effort.

Coconut Oil

Once demonized as artery-clogging sludge not fit to grease a doorframe, this tropical fat is now highly recommended by nutritionists. Touted for its benefits when consumed or used on the skin or hair, it's readily available just about anywhere you turn. Two varieties populate store shelves: virgin (also labeled as raw or unrefined) coconut oil and refined coconut oil. Virgin gets the best press from the health experts because it's less processed and bears the subtle aroma of the coconut flesh. Refined is wonderful for baked goods, however, since it has been deodorized and is essentially flavorless, allowing it to blend seamlessly into any dish. They both solidify below 76°F (24°C), but virgin oil reaches its smoke point at 350°F (180°C), while refined is at 450°F, meaning you can safely use it to fry or roast food at much higher temperatures. Either works fine for raw or unbaked applications, so feel free to choose one based on how much you want to taste the coconut essence in the final product.

Confectioner's Sugar

Otherwise known as powdered sugar, icing sugar, or 10x sugar, confectioner's sugar is a very finely ground version of standard white sugar, often with a touch of starch included to prevent clumping. You can make your own confectioner's sugar by powdering 1 cup of granulated sugar with 1 tablespoon of cornstarch in your food processor or spice grinder. Simply blend the sugar and cornstarch on the highest speed for about 2 minutes, allowing the dust to settle before opening your machine—unless you want to inhale a cloud of sugar!

Cream Cheese

Many innovative companies now make dairy-free products that will give you the most authentic shmears and cream cheese frostings imaginable. These soft spreads also hold up beautifully in cookie dough and piecrusts, contributing a great tangy flavor and excellent structure. This ingredient is hard to replace with homemade varieties when seeking smooth, consistent results, so I suggest that you check out your local mega mart or natural food grocer, or head online if all else fails.

Flaxseeds

Ground flaxseeds make an excellent vegan egg replacer when combined with water. One tablespoon of the whole seeds produces approximately 1½ tablespoons of the ground powder. While you can purchase preground flaxseed meal in many stores, I prefer to grind them fresh for each recipe, as they tend to go rancid much more quickly once broken down. Not to mention, it takes mere seconds to powder your own flaxseeds in a spice grinder. If you do opt to purchase flax meal instead, be sure to store the powder in your refrigerator or freezer until you are ready to use it. These tiny seeds can be found in bulk bins and prepackaged in the baking aisle of natural food stores.

Garlic

Quite possibly the single most celebrated seasoning the world over, garlic itself needs no explanation. Such popularity, however, has given rise to a wide range of garlicky options, some better suited for various recipes than others. There's no standard size for a clove of garlic, but a good rule of thumb is that, on average, one clove will yield about 1 teaspoon, minced. Granulated or powdered garlic is a bit more concentrated, so you can generally substitute ¼ to ½ teaspoon per clove if you're out of the fresh stuff, or simply want the distinctive flavor without the raw bite. You can also find prepared, already minced or pureed garlic both in shelf-stable jars and frozen packets for super-speedy cooking needs.

Graham Crackers

When I first went searching for vegan graham crackers, I was appalled at my lack of options. Why every brand in sight needed to include honey was beyond me. So, what is an intrepid food enthusiast to do in a tight situation like this? Shop, search, and browse some more, of course. Concealed among the rest, and often in natural foods stores, there are a few brands that exclude all animal products. Believe it or not, some of the best options are the store brand biscuits that may otherwise get overlooked. Keep your eyes peeled for unexpected steals and deals.

Granulated Sugar

Yes, plain old, regular white sugar. Surprised to see this basic sweetener here? It's true that all sugar (beet or cane) is derived from plant sources and therefore vegan by nature. However, there are some sneaky things going on behind the scenes in big corporations these days. Some cane sugar is filtered using bone char, a very non-vegan process, but that will never be specified on a label. If you're not sure about the brand that you typically buy, your best bet is to contact the manufacturer directly and ask.

To bypass this problem, many vegans purchase unbleached cane sugar. While it is a suitable substitute, unbleached cane sugar does have a higher molasses content than white sugar, so it has more of a brown sugar–like flavor and tends to produce desserts that are denser. Luckily, there are a few caring companies that go to great pains to ensure the purity of their sugar products, such as Florida Crystals and Amalgamated Sugar Company. I typically opt for one of these vegan sugar brands to get the best results. You can often find appropriate sugar in health food store bulk bins these days to save some money, but as always, verify the source before forking over the cash. As sugar can be a touchy vegan subject, it is best to use your own judgment when considering which brand to purchase.

Hemp Seeds

Yes, these are edible seeds from the *Cannabis sativa* plant, but unlike the leaves, they won't get you high. Instead, they're a concentrated source of omega-3 fatty acids and many other vital nutrients, which has bolstered their nutritional profile in recent years. Dubbed a "superfood" by many, these tiny kernels have a deeply savory, nutty flavor that blends nicely into both sweet and savory applications. Most hemp seeds are sold hulled, to make them a bit easier on the digestion, and are often squirreled away among the dietary supplements or in bulk bins.

Instant Coffee Powder or Granules

Though generally unfit for drinking as intended, instant coffee is an ideal way to add those crave-worthy roasted, smoky notes to any recipe without also incorporating a lot of extra liquid. Stored in a dry, dark place, a small jar should last a long time. You can even find decaf versions, in case you're more sensitive to caffeine but still want that flavor in your recipes. I prefer powder to granules because it dissolves more easily, but both can work interchangeably with a bit of vigorous mixing.

Jackfruit

Practically unheard of just a few years ago, jackfruit has taken the world by storm for its uncanny ability to imitate the texture of shredded meat. This tropical fruit can grow to gigantic proportions, easily exceeding 80 pounds, and its spiny exterior makes it quite a sight to behold. You're much more likely to encounter it canned, which is a merciful thing because its latex-like interior is a real pain to break down, coating everything from your knife to

your hands in stubbornly sticky goo. Always make sure you're purchasing young (or "immature") green jackfruit in brine, NOT in syrup. The sweetened stuff is objectively dreadful.

Maple Syrup

There is simply no substitute for real, 100 percent maple syrup. The flavor is like nothing else out there, and I have yet to meet a single brand of pancake syrup that could even come close. Of course, this incredible indulgence does come at a hefty price. Though it would be absolute sacrilege to use anything but authentic grade B maple syrup on pancakes or waffles in my house, I will sometimes bend the rules in recipes where it isn't such a prominent flavor, in order to save some money. In these instances, I'll substitute with a maple-agave blend, which still carries the flavor from the actual source, but bulks it up with an equal dose of agave for sweetening power. Grade A is a fine substitute in a pinch, but contrary to what the letter would suggest, it's actually less flavorful than grade B.

Mayonnaise

I was raised to believe that mayonnaise was the devil incarnate by my father, who absolutely despised

the stuff. That's why I never even tasted it before going vegan, and now I simply can't get enough of this sandwich spread. Without eggs, it's typically made from emulsified oils and pea or soy protein. It works well as a binder or base for creamy dressings, dipping sauces, and so much more. It keeps brilliantly in the fridge for months, so I always try to have some on hand. Although you can find some brands in the shelf-stable aisle of the grocery store (which must still be chilled after opening), I find that the best flavor comes from those sold refrigerated. You can find all sorts of options if you want one that's soy-free, organic, and more.

Miso Paste

Fermented soybeans coarsely ground and mixed with water sounds like a sad excuse for soup, yet it's the single most celebrated starter for any Japanese meal, be it breakfast, lunch, or dinner. The length of time that the beans are fermented determines the color and flavor of the finished paste; traditional miso is aged for at least 3 to 5 years, yielding a very dark, robust, and salty base. Lighter, gentler miso is often called "sweet" miso, which is delicious used as a condiment, spread very thinly on an ear of roasted corn, for example. Those sensitive to soy can now find many alternatives, the most common being chickpea miso, which more closely mimics the flavor of a light or white miso paste. Though all types can be substituted with more or less success, no two misos are exactly alike, and any changes can drastically alter the end results.

Nondairy Milk

The foundation of many cream and custard pies, this critical ingredient is left somewhat ambiguous for a reason. Most types of nondairy milk will work in these recipes, which leaves the possibilities wide open for anyone that needs to accommodate allergies or intolerances. Unless explicitly specified, any other type of vegan milk substitute will work. My top pick is unsweetened almond milk because it tends to be a bit thicker and richer but still has a neutral flavor. Don't be afraid to experiment, though; there's a lot to choose from!

Nutritional Yeast

Unlike active yeast, nutritional yeast is not used to leaven baked goods, but to flavor all sorts of dishes. Prized for its distinctly cheesy flavor, it's a staple in most vegan pantries and is finally starting to gain recognition in mainstream cooking as well. Though nutritional yeast is almost always found in savory recipes, I sometimes like to add a tiny pinch to some desserts, bringing out its subtle buttery characteristics. It can be found either in the baking aisle or in many bulk bin sections.

Salt

The importance of salt cannot be overstated. It's that spark that makes flavors pop and balances out spice mixtures that might otherwise overwhelm the palate. To make a long story short, you do not want to leave out this unassuming but critical ingredient! Unless otherwise noted, I use regular old table salt (finely ground) in baking. Flaky sea salt or kosher salt can be fun to sprinkle directly over finished baked goods before serving for an extra punch of flavor, but be careful not to overdo it; there's a fine line between salted and downright salty.

Seitan

All hail seitan! No, there's no demon worship going on here, and in fact, seitan originated on the opposite end of that spectrum. Buddhist monks first invented this "wheat meat" in ancient China, long before there was even a word for vegetarianism. Seitan is pure gluten, the stuff of celiac nightmares, but of bodybuilding dreams. Ounce for ounce, seitan has the same amount of protein as lean ground beef, and of course, less fat and no cholesterol. Textures range from chewy to spongy to pleasantly sinewy, depending on how it's sliced and cooked. Ready-to-use, prepared seitan can be found in health food stores alongside the packages of refrigerated tofu.

Sour Cream

Another creative alternative comes to the rescue of vegan eaters everywhere! Vegan sour cream provides an amazingly similar yet dairy-free version of the original tangy spread. In a pinch, I suppose you might be able to get away with using soy yogurt instead, but that is generally much thinner, so I really wouldn't recommend it. Vegan sour cream is sold in the refrigerated section of natural food stores and some mainstream grocers. It can often be found neatly tucked in among its dairy-based rivals, or with the other refrigerated dairy alternatives.

Speculoos

Crisp like gingersnaps but redolent of cinnamon rather than ginger, these brown sugar cookies can be spiced heavily or lightly, rolled thick or thin, and used as an ingredient or finished treat by themselves. No two bakers' speculoos will taste the same, but I prefer a mild cookie that is perfectly engineered for dipping into a cup of steaming coffee or hot chocolate. If you lack access to this crisp Belgian treat, graham crackers sprinkled with a bit of cinnamon can suffice in a pinch.

Sprinkles

What's a birthday party without a generous handful of sprinkles to brighten up the cake? Though these colorful toppers are made primarily of edible wax, they are often coated in confectioner's glaze, which is code for mashed-up insects, to give them their lustrous shine. Happily, you can now find specifically vegan sprinkles in both chocolate and colored versions, which can be found at just about any natural food store.

Sriracha

True heat-seekers and hot sauce fanatics may scoff at the relatively mild spice of sriracha, but that very quality is what makes it such a winning condiment for enhancing all cuisines. Leaning more heavily on garlic and a balanced sweetness than just pure fire power, it's dangerously easy to power through even the largest bottles available. Don't hold back, just enjoy the blaze; it's dirt cheap and found literally everywhere, even in gas stations and truck stops.

Tahini

An irreplaceable staple in Middle Eastern cuisine, tahini is a paste very much like peanut butter, but made from sesame seeds rather than nuts. If you don't have any on hand and a trip to the market is not in your immediate plans, then any other nut butter will provide exactly the same texture within a recipe, though it will impart a different overall taste. You can also make your own, just like you would make nut butter, but a high-speed blender is highly recommended to achieve a smooth texture. Tahini is sold at most regular grocery stores.

Tempeh

Tempeh is often compared to tofu because it's another high-protein soy product, but that's pretty much where the similarities end. Much more strongly flavored than tofu, tempeh is made from whole beans, and sometimes grains and even seeds, which are bound together in a fermented cake. Good bacteria cultures like those found in yogurt are the catalyst for this slow transformation, which makes it particularly high in vitamin B12 and beneficial for gut health. Raw tempeh can be somewhat bitter, which is why it's best cooked over high heat with equally assertive marinades. Although there are many different varieties available, they can all be used interchangeably.

Tofu

No longer the posterchild for flavorless vegetarian cookery, tofu is enjoying greater acceptance than ever as a highly versatile protein in its own right, rather than merely a bland meat substitute. For entrées where the tofu is chopped, sliced, or cubed, you should seek out firm, extra-firm, or even super-firm, water-packed varieties than can hold their own when the heat is on. Medium or firm are better for crumbled applications, and soft or silken is most appropriate for creamy purees, such as sauces, smoothies, and puddings. When I use tofu for baked goods and ice creams, I always reach for the aseptic, shelf-stable packs. Not only do they seem to last forever when unopened, but they also blend down into a perfectly smooth liquid when processed thoroughly, not a trace of grit or off-flavors to be found. Water-packed varieties can be stored for up to a month unopened, or 1 week if stored in an airtight container in the fridge, covered in fresh water that's changed every 2 or 3 days.

Vanilla (Extract, Paste, and Beans)

One of the most important ingredients in a baker's arsenal, vanilla is found in countless forms and qualities. It goes without saying that artificial flavorings pale in comparison to the real thing. Madagascar vanilla is the traditional full-bodied vanilla that most people appreciate in desserts, so stick with that and you can't go wrong. Happily, it's also the most common and moderately priced variety. To take your desserts up a step, vanilla paste brings in the same amount of flavor, but includes those lovely little vanilla bean flecks that makes everyone think you busted out the good stuff and used whole beans.

Vanilla paste can be substituted 1:1 for vanilla extract. Like whole vanilla beans, save the paste for things where you'll really see those specks of vanilla goodness, like ice creams, custards, and frostings.

Vanilla beans, the most costly but flavorful option, can be used instead, at about 1 bean per 2 teaspoons of extract or paste.

Once you've split and scraped out the insides, don't toss that vanilla pod! Get the most for your money by stashing it in a container of granulated sugar, to slowly infuse the sugar with delicious vanilla flavor. Alternatively, just store the pod in a container until it dries out, and then grind it up very finely in a high-speed blender and use it to augment a good vanilla extract. The flavor won't be nearly as strong as the seeds, but it does contribute to the illusion that you've used the good stuff.

Vegetable Stock

Be it brothy or creamy, thick or thin, a soup is only as good as its stock. Stock can be made up of absolutely any vegetables, but the most common ingredients are onions, carrots, and celery, at bare minimum. The trouble with commercial, ready-made options is that

Wasabi Paste and Powder

Just like the mounds of green paste served with sushi, the prepared wasabi paste found in tubes is almost certainly not made of wasabi root. Strange but true. It's typically colored horseradish instead, due to the rarity and expense of real wasabi. Read labels carefully, because it's one of those things that seems guaranteed to be vegan-friendly, but can give you a nasty surprise if you're not careful. Milk derivatives are often added, for reasons I couldn't begin to explain. Wasabi powder can be potent stuff indeed, but only if it's extremely fresh. The flavor dissipates over time, so be sure to toss any that has been sitting in your pantry well past its prime. If quality paste is nowhere to be found, opt for prepared horseradish (blended only with a dash of vinegar) instead. In some cases, mustard powder can lend a similar flavor instead of wasabi powder, but only in very small doses.

Yogurt

Fermented by good bacteria that are said to improve your digestion, yogurt now comes in just about any flavor, color, and nondairy formulation you can imagine. Soy, almond, coconut, and even cashew yogurts are readily available at most markets these days, and you can even find some that are agave sweetened. Double-check that whatever you decide to buy is certified as vegan; just because it's nondairy doesn't mean it uses vegan cultures. The big, multi-serving tubs are handy if you eat a lot of the stuff to begin with, but I generally prefer to purchase single-serving, 6-ounce containers for specific uses to avoid leftovers that may go bad too soon. Please note, however, that one container of yogurt does not equal 1 cup; 6 ounces is equivalent to ¾ cup by volume measure. It does help to have a food scale if you decide to buy in bulk to weigh out the exact amount that would be found in one standard container.

most lean too heavily on salt, throwing the carefully balanced seasoning of a dish out of whack. Always seek out low-sodium or no-salted-added varieties whenever possible, and read labels carefully to avoid artificial flavorings or preservatives. My favorite pantry staple is actual dry vegetable stock powder, which can be added to water according to taste.

Vinegar

At any given time, there are at least five different types of vinegar kicking around my kitchen, and that's a conservative estimate. As with oil, vinegar can be made from all sorts of fruit, grains, and roots, each with their own distinctive twang. Some, like white vinegar, rice vinegar, and apple cider vinegar, are fairly neutral and mild; others, such as balsamic vinegar and red wine vinegar, are far more assertive. The type you choose can radically change the character of the finished dish, which is why they all have a place in my pantry. Feel free to experiment with different varieties for a change of pace if you're open to new flavor adventures. In a pinch, you might also be able to get away with using fresh lemon or lime juice for a similar acidic punch.

ESSENTIAL SCHOOL SUPPLIES

Residence hall cooking means employing as few fancy kitchen tools and toys as possible, both out of necessity and for the sake of reducing the number of dirty dishes to wash afterward. If you live in an apartment instead of a residence hall, chances are you, too, have a small kitchen with limited space and supplies. At bare minimum, you'll need a few large bowls, a knife, a saucepan, a working stove or hot plate, and a microwave. While all the rest is optional, a few extra gadgets will certainly make the work move along more easily. The following suggestions are a few options that may aid in your culinary adventures.

Blender

Blenders come in all shapes and sizes, with wildly varying prices to match. A professional-grade, high-speed model would certainly be nice, but you can find perfectly serviceable options at all price points. Just look for something that can hold at least 4 to 6 cups of liquid, to accommodate soups and smoothies alike.

Hot Plate or Electric Burner

If you don't have access to a full stove, your next best bet is a portable, miniature burner. This may or may not be legal depending on your specific residence hall rules, so make sure they're allowed before hauling this one out in full view of your residence advisor. You want one that's electric so you can easily plug it in and start cooking, rather than one powered by butane, created with camping in mind. You can find highly affordable options starting from $20 and up, ranging from 1200 to 1800 watts; aim for something generally in the middle of that range to prevent the frustration of an underpowered element that can barely boil water. Only use it on a hard, sturdy surface, and keep it far away from the walls or anything potentially flammable. Always keep pot holders nearby, and you do know where the fire extinguisher is, right?

Knives

Every chef will agree that the single most important tool in the kitchen, aside from your hands, is a knife. Keep it sharp, clean, and safely stored, and it will never do you wrong. If you only have one knife, invest in a chef's knife or Japanese santoku between 7 and 8 inches (17.5 to 20 cm) long. You can find lightweight ceramic knives in very affordable sets that are razor sharp, too. Just bear in mind that they can be a bit more fragile than hardened steel, so don't try using them to crack open coconuts or anything else crazy.

Only use your knives on a cutting board, as tempting as it may be to just slice something up really quick on the counter. Not only will you damage the counter, but you'll also degrade your knife much faster, leading to a dull, unsatisfying blade. Bamboo or plastic cutting boards are your best bet for materials that are resilient but also easy to wash. Bear in mind that bamboo is more porous, and could stain if you use it to cut up beets or fresh turmeric.

Microwave

Did you know that the first microwave ever built was 6 feet tall, weighed 750 pounds, and cost $5,000? Vast technological advances have brought down all of those figures significantly, allowing the machines to become ubiquitous kitchen staples today. Few people give their microwaves a second thought, but different models can vary greatly in power and capacity. The average electromagnetic oven has an output of 700 watts, which is what most recipes are written to accommodate. If you're not sure about your own microwave, place a cup of water in a dish and see how long it takes to boil. For a 700 watt model, it should take about 2½ minutes; 1000 watts will get you there in only 1¾ minutes. Rarely will you encounter a noncommercial machine that pumps out over 1200 watts, which will boil water in under 1½ minutes. Once you harness the full power of your machine, adjust your cooking times accordingly. You can also find a more thorough conversion chart at MicrowaveWatt.com.

Mini Fridge

Although you can cook complete meals with only canned and shelf-stable ingredients, having a fridge to store fresh food gives you a lot more options. It also allows you to store your leftovers, so you can cook one meal and have dinner for the next night as well. Many residence halls these days come equipped with mini refrigerators, but if yours doesn't, consider investing in one. They cost $100 to $150 new, and you can get one for even less if you buy it secondhand. Hit up Craigslist, NextDoor, or Facebook Marketplace for some hot (er, cold) deals. When you graduate, you can resell it to another aspiring residence hall cook and get back a good chunk of what you paid.

Sauté Pan, Saucepan, and/or Skillet

Buying a full set of pans is awfully tempting. You can go from zero to fully equipped with a single click, everything on your stove top will match, and maybe they'll even stack neatly when you put them away. You could also put a whole pricey set on a wedding registry and hope that some big spender is feeling generous. However, it's money that is best put toward quality ingredients instead. You only need a few basics to cook pretty much everything, and it also means you'll have fewer dishes to wash at the end of the day. Go for an accommodating vessel, at least 12 inches (30.5 cm) wide, be it ceramic, nonstick, or stainless steel. Something with a heavy bottom to hold in the heat is best, and look for high sides if you want to make saucier or soupier items. Believe it or not, you can often find quality items at discounted home goods stores. Used pots and pans are not the greatest idea, as the coating can be scratched or worn, which is liable to flake off into your food. That's a seasoning I'd rather skip, personally.

Spatula

It's almost unfair to have just one category for all spatulas because it encompasses so many options. If you only have one, a silicone spatula is a must for blending pancake batter, incorporating ingredients for sticky bread doughs, stirring soups and stews, and making sure nothing sticks when making stir-fries. Heatproof and nearly indestructible, you can use them on dishes hot or cold without fear.

Spiralizer

Once an esoteric uni-tasking tool used exclusively in raw cuisine, spiralizers have taken the whole world by storm, spinning out curly strands of vegetables with the flick of the wrist. Operated much like a hand-crank pencil sharpener, spiralizers turn firm fruits and vegetables through a series of small blades to make "noodles" or ribbons of various sizes. Zucchini are typically the gateway drug for more daring plant-based pasta facsimiles; I've had wonderful results with seedless cucumbers, carrots, beets, strips of pumpkin, daikon, and parsnips, to name a few. You can find spiralizers for $15 to $40, and you don't need to splurge, since they're more or less just as effective. If you're not quite ready to commit, you can get a similar result from a julienne peeler, but it will take a bit more time and labor to turn out the same volume of skinny strands.

Strainer

When I call for one of these in a recipe, chances are I'm not talking about a pasta colander, with its large, spread-out holes. To sieve out raspberry seeds, drain vegan yogurt, or take care of any other liquid/solid separation jobs, a decent fine-mesh sieve will tackle the job with ease. Seek out strainers with solid construction, so that the mesh won't pull out after repeated pressings with a spatula. One that is 7 to 9 inches (17.5 to 23 cm) in diameter should accommodate.

LIFE LESSONS

Following a recipe is not rocket science. You don't need a degree in astrophysics to master your microwave. That said, there are a few simple techniques that will help you become more efficient and confident in the kitchen. Consider this a quick refresher course in cooking 101.

How to Use a Recipe

Though it may seem obvious, many people don't actually use recipes the right away, and wonder why their results don't match up to the glossy photos. First off, you need to read the recipe all the way through, from the ingredients to the instructions, before pulling out a single pot or pan. Make sure all the vegetables are prepped accordingly and ready to go. You want to know what you're doing before you have to do it, and make sure you actually have everything you need to make it, too!

How to Slice and Dice

While anyone can pick up a knife and immediately accomplish some serious plant-based butchery, it's equally as important to hone your knife skills as it is to keep your blade sharp. If you're not quite confident breaking down basic vegetables, hit up YouTube and find an endless trove of helpful visual assistance. More crucial than the actual cut, however,

is consistency. Keep all pieces uniformly the same size to ensure proper, even cooking. As they say, practice makes perfect; cook more often and you'll cook better overall!

How to Bake a Potato

Adaptable, affordable, and always accessible, a baked potato can be a side dish or respectable main in its own right, given the right kind of toppings. It can take 50 to 60 minutes in the oven, but you can cut that time down by a fraction if you pop it into the microwave instead. Pierce the spud all over with a fork and zap for 5 minutes, turn, and cook for 3 to 5 minutes more, until fully tender. Handle with care, as it will be steaming hot!

How to Toast Nuts, Seeds, and Coconut

Microwaves are my preferred appliance when it comes to toasting nuts, seeds, and coconut in the blink of an eye. Spread out the ingredients in an even layer on a large plate, leaving the center clear (since it tends to cook less evenly). Heat for 1 to 3 minutes, depending on the particular ingredient and quantity, stirring every 30 seconds or so to ensure an even, golden roast. It tends to move very quickly from raw to burnt, so you must keep a close eye on the process from start to finish.

How to Make a Vinaigrette

Ditch the store-bought bottles in favor of something fresher. All you need to make a basic dressing is oil and vinegar. Herbs and spices will help jazz things up, and don't be afraid to try different acidic additions; lemon or lime juice is just as invigorating! Start with the vinegar or acid in a medium bowl and slowly drizzle in the oil, whisking constantly, until incorporated. Even if the emulsion breaks, don't worry about it. Simply shake well before each use.

How to Clean Greens

Sure, you could buy prewashed, precut greens for ease, but you'll get a much better bang for your buck if you go straight to the source. Fresh greens are notoriously dirty diamonds, so you should always wash them thoroughly before use. Just fill a large bowl or your kitchen sink with cold water. Separate the greens and add them, vigorously swirling the water and agitating the greens. If you are washing whole heads of greens, dunk the heads and gently open them up, bending the leaves away from the core to allow water to get in between the leaves and remove the dirt stuck there. Dry in a salad spinner, and/or pat dry with paper towels.

How to Cook Pasta

Perfect pasta is within everyone's grasp once you understand the basics! Bring the water to a full rolling boil over high heat before you add the pasta. Add a hefty pinch of salt to season the pasta, and skip the oil. Contrary to conventional lore, it won't prevent the pasta from sticking. Add the pasta and immediately stir to prevent it from all cooking together in a clump. Follow the timing guidance on the package, testing at the earlier stage. Remove one piece from the water and cut it in half. Pasta that offers resistance but has no trace of brittleness is called "al dente," which literally means "to the tooth" in Italian. If it's undercooked, you'll see a white dot or line clearly visible in the center. Toss it back in and keep cooking.

How to Make Toast

Of course, if you have a toaster, this one is covered, but you don't need special equipment to enjoy a crunchy, warm slice of bread on demand. You can make it in a skillet set over medium heat, either dry or with a tiny drop of oil. Cook for 3 to 5 minutes on each side until golden brown. Alternatively, you can pop the bread into your oven on the highest rack, and use the broiler setting on "high." Toast for 2 to 3 minutes on each side.

How to Measure

Getting the right amounts of ingredients is fundamental to any recipe. Though cooking does give you more wiggle room than baking, you should still stick as close to the original amounts for best results. For volume measurements, pour, sprinkle, or gently spoon dry ingredients into your measuring cup until it's slightly overfull. Never pack it down, and with flour or powdered sugar, never use the cup as a scoop. Use the straight edge of a butter knife or spatula to scrape the excess off the top, giving you a perfectly level, full measure. The exception to this rule is brown sugar, which should be packed down firmly to yield the intended amount. For liquid ingredients, set a clear glass measuring cup on a flat surface and bring yourself down to eye level to get a more accurate reading.

How to Juice Citrus

Sure, you could just buy bottled juice at the store for convenience and ease, but nothing compares to fresh citrus. No matter the fruit, you get the best yield when it's at room temperature. You could also microwave it for 20 seconds to make it softer and easier to squeeze. Roll gently but firmly on the counter to start breaking the cell walls before cutting it in half across the equator. Start by squeezing with your hands over a medium bowl to catch the liquid, and then use the tines of a fork to extract every last drop. Twist and squeeze until nothing comes out. Strain the liquid to remove any seeds.

How to Season to Taste

Taste is entirely subjective, which is why the final amounts of salt, pepper, and spice are entirely up to you. Wait until the dish is completely done cooking and cool enough to eat before adjusting, because the flavors can continue to evolve with heat and time. If you're cooking for other people, stick with the lesser amounts suggested and let them season their own dishes, so everyone's palate is pleased.

How to Melt Chocolate

First, make sure your chocolate is finely chopped if using a bar, or equally sized pieces if using chips. Place them in a clear glass bowl so you can see the melting in action. Then, microwave for 1 minute on high. The chocolate will look shiny; stir thoroughly. Microwave in 20-second intervals if unmelted pieces remain, stirring after each interval, until totally smooth.

CONVERSIONS AND EQUIVALENTS

US DRY VOLUME MEASUREMENTS

Measure	Equivalent
¹⁄₁₆ teaspoon	Dash
⅛ teaspoon	Pinch
3 teaspoons	1 tablespoon
⅛ cup	2 tablespoons (also equivalent to 1 standard coffee scoop)
¼ cup	4 tablespoons
⅓ cup	5 tablespoons + 1 teaspoon
½ cup	8 tablespoons
¾ cup	12 tablespoons
1 cup	16 tablespoons
1 pound	16 ounces

US TO METRIC CONVERSIONS

⅕ teaspoon	1 ml (ml stands for milliliter, or one-thousandth of a liter)
1 teaspoon	5 ml
1 tablespoon	15 ml
1 fluid ounce	30 ml
⅕ cup	50 ml
1 cup	240 ml
2 cups (1 pint)	470 ml
4 cups (1 quart)	0.95 liter
4 quarts (1 gallon)	3.8 liters
1 ounce	28 grams
1 pound	454 grams

US LIQUID VOLUME MEASUREMENTS

8 fluid ounces	1 cup
1 pint	2 cups (16 fluid ounces)
1 quart	2 pints (4 cups)
1 gallon	4 quarts (16 cups)
⅓ cup	5 tablespoons + 1 teaspoon
½ cup	8 tablespoons
¾ cup	12 tablespoons
1 cup	16 tablespoons
1 pound	16 ounces

METRIC TO US CONVERSIONS

1 ml	⅕ teaspoon
5 ml	1 teaspoon
15 ml	1 tablespoon
30 ml	1 fluid ounce
100 ml	3.4 fluid ounces
240 ml	1 cup
1 liter	34 fluid ounces
1 liter	4.2 cups
1 liter	2.1 pints
1 liter	1.06 quarts
1 liter	0.26 gallon
1 gram	0.035 ounce
100 grams	3.5 ounces
500 grams	1.10 pounds
1 kilogram	2.205 pounds
1 kilogram	35 ounces

MEASURES FOR PANS AND DISHES

9 x 13-inch baking dish	22 x 33-centimeter baking dish
8 x 8-inch baking dish	20 x 20-centimeter baking dish
9 x 5-inch loaf pan	23 x 12-centimeter loaf pan (8 cups or 2 liters in capacity)
10-inch tart or cake pan	25-centimeter tart or cake pan
9-inch cake pan	22-centimeter cake pan
1 cup	240 ml
2 cups (1 pint)	470 ml
4 cups (1 quart)	0.95 liter
4 quarts (1 gallon)	3.8 liters
1 ounce	28 grams
1 pound	454 grams

OVEN TEMPERATURE CONVERSIONS

Fahrenheit	Celsius	Gas Mark
275°F	140°C	gas mark 1—cool
300°F	150°C	gas mark 2
325°F	165°C	gas mark 3—very moderate
350°F	180°C	gas mark 4—moderate
375°F	190°C	gas mark 5
400°F	200°C	gas mark 6—moderately hot
425°F	220°C	gas mark 7—hot
450°F	230°C	gas mark 9
475°F	240°C	gas mark 10—very hot

MEASURE EQUIVALENTS

Butter			
1 tablespoon	14 grams		
1 stick	4 ounces (113 grams)	8 tablespoons	½ cup
4 sticks	16 ounces (452 grams)	32 tablespoons	2 cups
Lemon			
1 lemon	1–3 tablespoons juice	1–1½ teaspoons zest	
4 lemons	1 cup juice	1/4 cup zest	
Chocolate			
1 ounce	1/4 cup finely grated (40 grams)		
6 ounces chips	1 cup chips (160 grams)		
Cocoa Powder			
1 cup	115 grams		

LETTUCE
CILANTRO
BELL PEPPERS
TOMATOES
AVOCADOS
CORN ON THE COB
VEGETABLE STOCK
YELLOW CORNMEAL

Breakfast All Day

chapter 1

ALL-PURPOSE PANCAKES FOR ONE

Flexible, versatile, and made from simple pantry staples, these small-batch pancakes are perfect for treating yourself on a whim.

½ cup (60 g) all-purpose flour

1 teaspoon baking powder

¼ teaspoon baking soda

2 tablespoons (24 g) granulated sugar

Pinch of salt

½ cup (120 ml) plain nondairy milk

2 tablespoons (30 g) fruit puree (such as applesauce, mashed bananas, or pumpkin puree)

1 teaspoon olive oil

1. In a medium bowl, stir together the flour baking powder, baking soda, sugar, and salt.

2. In a second bowl, stir together the milk, fruit puree, and oil.

3. Add the wet ingredients to the dry and stir just enough to combine the two.

4. Lightly grease a skillet and turn up the heat to medium, making sure it has time to get hot before adding the batter.

5. When ready, ladle dollops of the batter into your skillet and allow them to sit, undisturbed, for 2 to 3 minutes, until bubbles appear along the top and the edges seem to have firmed up a bit.

6. Flip and cook for another 2 to 3 minutes on the other side. Transfer to a plate, eat, and watch your mood miraculously improve.

GRANOLA PANCAKES

Boost your breakfast by turning humble granola into a hearty, healthy stack of pancakes. Toasted oats, crunchy nuts, and sweet fruits are built right into this easy formula.

1 cup (120 g) all-purpose gluten-free flour blend or unbleached all-purpose flour

1 tablespoon (8 g) whole chia seeds, finely ground

1½ teaspoons baking powder

½ teaspoon ground cinnamon

¼ teaspoon salt

¾ cup (180 ml) plain nondairy milk

1 tablespoon (15 ml) maple syrup

1 tablespoon (15 ml) lemon juice

2 tablespoons (28 g) coconut oil, melted

½ cup (75 g) granola

1. In a large bowl, whisk together the flour, ground chia seeds, baking powder, cinnamon, and salt.

2. In a second bowl, mix together the nondairy milk, maple syrup, lemon juice, and melted coconut oil.

3. Pour the wet ingredients into the dry and whisk just enough to bring together a loose batter; it's perfectly fine to leave a few lumps remaining.

4. Place a large, flat skillet on the stove over medium heat. Lightly grease, and once the skillet is up to temperature, use a ¼-cup (60 ml) measure to drop dollops of batter in circles approximately 4 inches (10 cm) across. Don't crowd the pan; cook only 2 to 3 pancakes at a time.

5. Sprinkle a handful of granola across the raw surface of each pancake. Cook for 3 to 4 minutes, until the bottom is golden brown, before flipping. Cook for an additional 1 to 2 minutes, until the other side is evenly browned as well.

6. Transfer to a plate and repeat with the remaining batter and granola. Serve warm, with additional granola, maple syrup, and fruit.

ESSENTIAL EGGLESS CRÊPES

Delicate, gossamer-thin French crêpes can be made without butter, milk, or eggs. These classic pancakes take shape with simple plant-based pantry staples and just a little bit of finesse.

½ cup (60 g) all-purpose flour

½ cup (60 g) chickpea flour

2 tablespoons (24 g) granulated sugar

¼ teaspoon salt

1 cup (240 ml) plain nondairy milk

2 tablespoons (30 ml) olive oil

¼ cup (60 ml) aquafaba (see page 10)

1 to 2 tablespoons (15 to 30 ml) water

1. In a large bowl, stir together both flours, sugar, and salt just to distribute the dry ingredients evenly. Add the nondairy milk and olive oil, and whisk thoroughly to combine. You don't want leave any lumps, but don't go crazy and overdo it either. Let the mixture sit for 5 minutes, after which you may notice it will thicken slightly. Slowly add the aquafaba, a tablespoon at a time, to thin it to the consistency of melted ice cream. If it is still too thick, add the water to reach the desired consistency.

2. Place a nonstick skillet over medium heat, and grease very, very lightly. If you're using a spray, use a paper towel to wipe away any excess. Once the pan becomes hot enough, pour in ¼ cup (60 g) of the batter. The traditional method of shaping the crêpes is to swirl the pan around so that the batter drips into shape, but this never gave me satisfactory results—no matter how quickly I worked, the crêpes were always terribly misshapen. After a lot of trial and error, I found that using the bottom of the ¼ cup measuring cup to push the batter in a circle was much more effective, but if you use this technique, make sure that the cup is not plastic, as it could melt! Either way you choose to go about it, speed is key, because these cook very quickly.

3. Let the crêpe cook for 1 to 2 minutes on each side. You will know that the first side is done cooking because the top will start to look a bit dry. Use your spatula to go around the edges and loosen the crêpe first before flipping, to make sure all of it flips at once.

4. Do not re-grease the pan between crêpes, as the nonstick surface should continue to do its job just fine. The pan will continue to get hotter as you cook, so if you notice the crêpes browning too quickly, be sure to turn down the heat just a step. Stack finished crêpes on a plate and cover with a clean towel to keep warm before serving.

FREAKY GOOD FRENCH TOAST

When I first attempted French toast, it was still very early in my "career" as a vegan. Because I had yet to really move into my element in the kitchen, my whole family remained dubious of what could be done without milk or eggs. Still, I persevered and came up with this impossibly buttery, eggy, cinnamon-scented rendition with ease. All it took was one mouthful of this delicious dish for my skeptical loved ones to start thinking about veganism in an entirely different way.

4 slices whole wheat bread

2 tablespoons (16 g) whole wheat or all-purpose flour

1 teaspoon nutritional yeast

2 tablespoons (24 g) firmly packed dark brown sugar

¼ teaspoon salt

½ teaspoon ground cinnamon

Pinch of ground nutmeg

1 cup (240 ml) plain nondairy milk

2 teaspoons olive oil or vegan butter

1. Begin by lightly toasting your bread, making it bit firmer and more receptive to the extra moisture that you will be adding.

2. In a shallow pan, add the flour, nutritional yeast, brown sugar, salt, cinnamon, and nutmeg and whisk to combine.

3. Stir in the milk and allow it to sit for a minute or two. Whisk again before using, to ensure that no lumps are left behind.

4. Soak 2 pieces of toast in the mixture while heating up a skillet on the stove. Grease the pan lightly with oil or vegan butter.

5. Flip your toast over and let the wet mixture absorb into the other side for another minute or two.

6. Once they appear to be fully saturated, carefully lift the slices out with a large spatula and place them in the hot skillet over medium-high heat; fry for 3 to 5 minutes per side.

7. Once nicely browned and crisp on the outside, transfer the toast to a plate, and repeat the process with the remaining 2 bread slices. Serve with maple syrup, fruit spread, or powdered sugar as you see fit.

SPRING PEA TOAST

This combination of rich almond-based ricotta and bright pea puree on a slab of hearty, seeded bread is an easy recipe to make at home for a taste of spring that everyone can enjoy year-round, worldwide.

MINTED PEA SPREAD

½ cup (15 g) lightly packed fresh mint

1 cup (30 g) lightly packed fresh spinach

3 tablespoons (45 ml) olive oil

2 tablespoons (30 ml) lemon juice

1 pound (454 g) frozen green peas, thawed

½ teaspoon salt

¼ teaspoon ground black pepper

TO ASSEMBLE

1 cup (240 g) vegan cream cheese or ricotta

4 large, thick slices bread, toasted

½ cup (75 g) fresh peas

Pea shoots or sprouts, for garnish (optional)

1   To make the spread, place the mint, spinach, oil, and lemon juice in a food processor and blend until the leaves are all broken down like rough pesto. Pause to scrape down the sides of the bowl as needed to make sure everything gets incorporated. Add the peas, salt, and pepper, and pulse until coarsely chopped.

2. To assemble the toast, layer on a thick schmear of cream cheese on each slice of bread, followed by the pea spread and topped with fresh peas. Garnish with pea shoots, if desired. Savor a taste of spring, no matter the weather outside!

note

The pea spread can be prepared in advance and stored in an airtight container in the fridge for 3 to 4 days.

CARROT CAKE OATMEAL

Have your cake and eat it for breakfast, too! Satisfy your sweet tooth while fueling yourself for the day with a hearty bowl of lightly spiced and tender oats featuring the sweetness of classic carrot cake. The combination is so compelling, you won't even realize you're getting an extra serving of vegetables for breakfast.

1 (14-ounce [392 g]) can full-fat coconut milk

½ cup (40 g) steel-cut oats

½ cup (60 g) shredded carrots

¼ cup (38 g) raisins

2½ tablespoons (37 ml) maple syrup

½ teaspoon ground cinnamon

¼ teaspoon ground ginger

¼ teaspoon salt

2 tablespoons (18 g) chopped, toasted walnuts

¼ teaspoon vanilla extract

1. In a medium saucepan over medium heat, stir together the coconut milk, oats, carrots, raisins, maple syrup, cinnamon, ginger, and salt.

2. Cover, bring to a boil, lower the heat, and simmer gently for 25 to 30 minutes, until the oats are tender but still toothsome. If it seems a bit too thick or dry, add in a splash of water, as needed.

3. Stir walnuts and vanilla into the oatmeal and serve hot.

CHAI-SPICED OATMEAL

Wake up to the invigorating aroma of chai spices when you get these highly spiced oats on the stove in no time! Prep ahead to simply heat and eat when you're in a rush.

3½ cups (840 ml) plain nondairy milk

½ cup (70 g) raw cashews

1 cup (80 g) steel-cut oats

¼ cup (60 ml) maple syrup

1 teaspoon black tea leaves

1½ teaspoons ground ginger

1¼ teaspoons ground cinnamon

½ teaspoon salt

¼ teaspoon ground cloves

¼ teaspoon ground allspice

¼ teaspoon ground cardamom

1 teaspoon vanilla extract

1. Puree the nondairy milk and cashews in a blender until smooth.

2. Pour the mixture into a medium saucepan along with the oats, maple syrup, tea leaves, ginger, cinnamon, salt, cloves, allspice, and cardamom.

3. Cover, bring to a boil, and reduce the heat to low. Simmer for 25 to 30 minutes, until the oats are tender but still toothsome. If it seems a bit too thick or dry, add in a splash of water, as needed.

4. Stir in the vanilla and serve hot.

note

After cooking, the oatmeal can be refrigerated and stored for up to 5 days or portioned into individual ramekins and frozen for 3 to 4 months. When serving the oatmeal after freezing, allow it to fully thaw in the refrigerator overnight before heating in the microwave or on the stove top.

EGGLESS LENTIL SCRAMBLE

Scramble up a simple, hearty breakfast without using any tofu! Red lentils make this plant-powered meal even healthier, and arguably tastier, than the traditional eggless approach.

¾ cup (150 g) red lentils

1 teaspoon black salt (kala namak)

½ teaspoon onion powder

¼ teaspoon ground turmeric

1 tablespoon (6 g) nutritional yeast

1½ cups (360 ml) plain, unsweetened nondairy milk

2 tablespoons (28 g) butter-flavored coconut oil, melted

¼ cup (30 g) cassava flour

¾ teaspoon baking powder

1. Bring a large pot of water to a boil and add the lentils. Immediately turn off the heat, cover, and let soak for 30 minutes. Drain thoroughly.

2. Place the lentils in a blender along with the black salt, onion powder, turmeric, nutritional yeast, milk, coconut oil, flour, and baking powder. Blend on high speed until completely pureed, creamy, and smooth. The mixture should be the consistency of pancake batter—pourable but not soupy.

3. Transfer the mixture to a large nonstick or lightly greased skillet set over medium heat. Let cook for 2 to 3 minutes, undisturbed, until it begins to look slightly dry around the edges.

4. Use your spatula to push the mixture gently, slowly around the skillet, scraping the bottom to ensure that nothing sticks or burns. Continue scrambling until curds form and the entire mixture has set to your desired consistency. Stop sooner for soft scrambled eggs or keep it on the stove longer if you prefer them on the drier side.

5. Transfer to plates and serve hot.

PINK POMEGRANATE SMOOTHIE BOWL

Pretty in pink but powerfully nutritious, this easy blend will energize, satisfy, and soothe, all in one delicious spoonful.

2 frozen bananas, sliced

2 tablespoons (16 g) pitaya powder

2 to 4 tablespoons (30 to 60 ml) pomegranate juice

2 tablespoons (16 g)

pomegranate arils

1 tablespoon (8 g) goji berries or raisins

1 teaspoon hemp seeds

1. In a food processor, pulse the frozen banana, pitaya powder, and pomegranate juice to begin breaking down the fruit. Scrape down the sides of the bowl with a spatula periodically to keep everything incorporated.

2. Puree at full power until smooth and creamy. Add more juice as needed to achieve your desired consistency, and transfer to a bowl.

3. Arrange the pomegranate arils, goji berries, and hemp seeds on top of the mixture. Serve immediately.

note

Feel free to simplify this recipe or give it an extra nutritional boost by replacing the pitaya powder with your favorite protein powder. Neutral, vanilla, or berry-flavored blends would be the most harmonious here.

GOOD MORNING MANGO LASSI

Cool, creamy, and thoroughly refreshing, this morning yogurt drink is blended with juicy mango chunks.

1 cup (175 g) diced mango, fresh or frozen

½ cup (120 g) plain vegan yogurt

½ cup (120 ml) plain nondairy milk or coconut milk

1 tablespoon (15 ml) maple syrup

1 teaspoon lemon juice

¼ teaspoon ground cardamom (optional)

Pinch of salt

1. Simply toss the mango, yogurt, milk, maple syrup, lemon juice, cardamom (if using), and salt in your blender and thoroughly puree, until the mixture is completely smooth. You may need to pause and scrape down the sides of the container if you see any clumps of unblended ingredients clinging to the sides.

2. Serve immediately or chill for up to 2 hours before enjoying. The beverage may separate a bit if it sits, so stir thoroughly before serving.

note

Cardamom is a traditional flavoring but can be overwhelming for some, so feel free to either omit it entirely or substitute ground ginger for a different spicy experience.

ALMOND JOY MILKSHAKE

Leave the candy bars in the vending machine and opt for this decadent yet stunningly healthy shake instead! Toss it in a shaker bottle and enjoy it all through morning classes. Getting through the a.m. slog without your stomach growling is something to be truly joyful about.

1½ cups (360 ml) full-fat coconut milk

¼ cup (30 g) chocolate vegan protein powder

2 tablespoons (30 g) creamy almond butter

¼ teaspoon almond extract

1 to 2 tablespoons (15 to 30 ml) maple syrup

Sliced almonds, for garnish (optional)

1. Toss the milk, protein powder, almond butter, almond extract, and maple syrup in a blender and puree until completely smooth. Start with just 1 tablespoon (15 ml) of maple syrup, taste the mixture once blended, and see if it needs a little additional sweetness. Add the remaining 1 tablespoon (15 ml) if desired.

2. Serve immediately or chill for up to 2 hours before enjoying. Garnish the drink with a small pinch of sliced almonds for a bit of extra flare.

AVOCADO ICED COFFEE

Rich, creamy coffee with a touch of sweetness and not a drop of dairy! Serve over ice for maximum refreshment.

½ ripe avocado, peeled and pitted

½ cup (120 ml) full-fat coconut milk

¼ teaspoon vanilla extract

1 to 2 drops liquid stevia (see Note)

1 cup (240 ml) strong brewed coffee, cooled

Ice, to serve

1. In a blender, combine the avocado, milk, vanilla, stevia, and coffee until smooth.

2. Fill one or two glasses with ice, and pour the coffee mixture on top. Sip and savor!

note

Feel free to use your favorite sweetener here, be it maple syrup, coconut sugar, or good old granulated, to taste.

PUMPKIN PROTEIN POWER LATTE

For a bolder brew that will help wake you up and keep you going, consider pump-kin up the volume with this quick blend! Whether this latte is served hot or cold, sugary coffee shop concoctions just can't compete. For a more indulgent experience, consider topping off your mug with whipped coconut cream!

1 cup (240 ml) brewed coffee, hot or chilled

½ cup (120 ml) plain nondairy milk

½ cup (120 g) pumpkin puree

¼ cup (30 g) vanilla vegan protein powder

1 to 2 tablespoons (15 to 30 ml) maple syrup

½ teaspoon ground cinnamon

¼ teaspoon ground ginger

Pinch of ground cloves

Pinch of ground nutmeg

1. This protein-packed blend can be served either hot or cold, so depending on your preference, either cool down your coffee after brewing or use it right away and heat up your nondairy milk to match. Pour both into your blender along with all the remaining ingredients, adding only 1 tablespoon (15 ml) of maple syrup at first. Thoroughly puree, until the mixture is completely smooth, scraping down the sides of the container with a spatula if any clumps of unblended ingredients cling to the sides.

2. Taste the mixture and add the remaining 1 tablespoon (15 ml) maple syrup if you'd prefer a sweeter taste.

LETTUCE
CILANTRO
BELL PEPPERS
TOMATOES
AVOCADOS
CORN ON THE COB
VEGETABLE STOCK
YELLOW CORNMEAL

Incredible Dips, Spreads, and Sprinkles

chapter 2

Sooo good!

ALMOND PARMESAN

For the perfectly cheesy finishing touch, you'll want to keep this versatile savory sprinkle on hand at all times. it comes together in the blink of an eye and satisfies cravings in an instant.

1 cup (120 g) blanched almond meal

2 tablespoons (12 g) nutritional yeast

¼ teaspoon onion powder

¼ teaspoon salt

1. Mix everything together in a large bowl, stirring thoroughly to combine.

2. Use right away or store in an airtight container in the fridge for 2 to 3 weeks.

BUTTERNUT QUESO

Nothing starts a party (or study session) off right like a big bowl of spicy queso and plenty of tortilla chips for dipping. You could bring on the fire with diced jalapeños, a squirt of sriracha, or chipotle in adobo if you really like it hot!

2 cups (480 ml) unsweetened nondairy milk

8 ounces (227 g) butternut squash, peeled and diced

½ cup (70 g) raw cashews

¼ cup (24 g) nutritional yeast

1 teaspoon chili powder

1 teaspoon onion powder

1 teaspoon garlic powder

½ teaspoon ground cumin

½ teaspoon salt

1 Roma tomato, diced

1. Combine the nondairy milk, butternut squash, and cashews in a medium saucepan over medium heat. Bring to a boil, reduce the heat to a simmer, and cook until the butternut is fork-tender, 15 to 20 minutes.

2. Transfer to a blender and puree on high speed. Add the nutritional yeast, chili powder, onion powder, garlic powder, cumin, and salt and blend once more to incorporate. Fold in the tomato by hand to keep it chunky.

3. Pour into a serving bowl and enjoy warm!

note

No blender? No problem! Just use 1 cup of pumpkin puree instead of whole butternut chunks. Cook for just 5 to 8 minutes until thickened.

CHICKPEA FLOUR HUMMUS

Thrifty, resourceful, and most importantly, delicious, hummus is a universally beloved dip. Nothing can stop me from getting my legume love, which is why I always have plenty of chickpea flour in the pantry. Yes, you can turn it into luscious, creamy bean dip, too! The super smooth texture gives canned beans a run for their money.

2½ to 3 cups (600 to 720 ml) vegetable stock or water

¼ cup (60 ml) lemon juice

¾ cup (90 g) chickpea flour

3 cloves garlic, finely minced, or 1½ teaspoons garlic powder

½ teaspoon ground cumin

¼ teaspoon ground coriander

¼ to ½ teaspoon salt

¼ teaspoon ground black pepper

¼ cup (60 g) tahini

¼ cup (60 ml) olive oil

1. In a medium saucepan over medium heat, whisk together 2½ cups (600 ml) of the stock, lemon juice, chickpea flour, garlic, cumin, coriander, salt, and pepper. Slowly bring to a boil, whisking gently but continuously, until thickened to the consistency of pancake batter, 8 to 10 minutes.

2. Whisk in the tahini and olive oil, and cook for just another minute, until smooth and fully incorporated.

3. The mixture will continue to thicken as it cools; allow at least 30 minutes before serving. Adjust the salt to taste, and thin with more stock or water if desired. Eat warm or chilled.

notes

In times of scarcity or boredom, these ratios can withstand some creative substitutions:

* Instead of chickpea flour, use green pea flour or lentil flour.

* Instead of lemon juice, use lime juice or rice vinegar.

* Instead of tahini, use cashew butter or peanut butter.

* Instead of olive oil, use avocado oil or melted coconut oil.

* Instead of these spices, use any of your favorite blends.

CHUNKY BABA GANOUSH

I love baba ganoush, but sometimes it's just a bit too much like baba gaMUSH, if you know what I mean. While there's nothing wrong with a completely creamy puree, I do enjoy a dip with a bit more texture. By going low-tech and skipping the food processor, you get a much more satisfying bite, with fewer dishes to clean.

2 medium Italian eggplants (about 2½ pounds total)

¼ cup (60 g) tahini

2 tablespoons (30 ml) olive oil

2 tablespoons (30 ml) lemon juice

1 clove garlic, minced

½ teaspoon salt

2 tablespoons (8 g) minced parsley

1. Set a medium skillet over high heat and place the eggplants directly in the dry pan. Use tongs to rotate the eggplants every 6 to 8 minutes, until the skin is charred all over.

2. Place the eggplants in a large bowl and cover with plastic wrap, allowing them to steam. Once completely cool, peel away the skin, and then coarsely chop the flesh.

3. Transfer the flesh to a bowl and stir in the tahini, olive oil, lemon juice, garlic, salt, and parsley. Serve at room temperature or thoroughly chilled.

4. Store leftovers in the fridge in an airtight container for up to 5 days.

Quick + Cheap

COCONUT BACON

Crunchy, smoky, savory, and subtly sweet strips of coconut create an unbelievably satisfying substitute for bacon bits. Use them to top everything from salads to pasta, soups to sandwiches, and beyond.

2 cups (160 g) coconut flakes

1 tablespoon (15 ml) olive oil

1 tablespoon (15 ml) soy sauce

1 tablespoon (15 ml) maple syrup

2 teaspoons (10 ml) apple cider vinegar

1 teaspoon liquid smoke

1 teaspoon smoked paprika

½ teaspoon salt

1. Preheat the oven to 300°F (150°C, or gas mark 2) and line a baking sheet with parchment paper or a silicone baking mat.

2. Place coconut flakes in a large bowl, add the oil, soy sauce, maple syrup, vinegar, liquid smoke, paprika, and salt. Mix well to ensure even and thorough coverage. Use your hands to gently massage the mixture, separating out the flakes and getting the marinade fully infused into the flakes.

3. Spread the coconut in a very thin layer on the prepared baking sheet, separating the pieces to the best of your ability.

4. Bake for 12 to 15 minutes, stirring every 3 to 5 minutes to prevent the pieces from burning at the edges. When fully baked, the coconut will darken in color but may not be fully crisp.

5. Remove from the oven and let cool completely; the coconut should become perfectly dry and crunchy crisp upon cooling.

FUNFETTI DUNKAROO DIP

If you're the type of person who would rather eat the frosting than the cake, then this dessert dip is for you! It's perfect for taming last-minute sugar cravings without blowing your budget on fancy bakery treats.

1 (8-ounce [227 g]) package vegan cream cheese

5 tablespoons (70 g) vegan butter

2 cups (240 g) confectioner's sugar

2 teaspoons (10 ml) vanilla extract

½ cup (60 g) rainbow sprinkles, divided

Animal crackers or graham crackers, to serve

1. In a large bowl, beat together the cream cheese and vegan butter until smooth.

2. Add the confectioner's sugar and vanilla, and stir vigorously for 3 to 5 minutes, until homogenous, light, and fluffy. Scrape down the sides of the bowl periodically to make sure that everything is fully incorporated.

3. Set aside about 2 tablespoons (15 g) of the sprinkles, and gently fold in the rest.

4. Transfer the dip to a serving dish and top with the reserved sprinkles. Serve with animal or graham crackers, and dip to your heart's content!

GUACAMOLE

When guacamole meets mole, the results may not be pretty, but the flavor is out of this world. This creamy, smoky, spicy, and earthy mash-up will tempt you to double (or triple) dip.

2 tablespoons (16 g) unsweetened cocoa powder

1 teaspoon ground cumin

1 teaspoon chipotle powder

¼ teaspoon ground nutmeg

¼ teaspoon ground cinnamon

¼ teaspoon ground cloves

¼ teaspoon salt

⅛ teaspoon ground white pepper

2 avocados

2 tablespoons (30 ml) lime juice

1 medium Roma tomato, chopped

2 cloves garlic, finely minced

2 tablespoons (2 g) minced fresh cilantro

2 scallions, thinly sliced

1. In a medium bowl, combine the cocoa, cumin, chipotle powder, nutmeg, cinnamon, cloves, salt, and pepper and mix well.

2. Pit, dice, and scoop the avocado flesh out, adding it to the bowl along with the lime juice. Very roughly mash with a fork, incorporating all the dry ingredients but keeping the texture rather chunky.

3. Mix in the tomato, garlic, cilantro, and scallions last, stirring until the vegetables and herbs are equally distributed throughout the dip.

4. Serve with chips or cut vegetable crudités.

PARTY!!!

SPICY TU-NO SUSHI SPREAD

Enjoy crunchy mouthfuls of sushi-inspired spicy "tuna" made with chickpeas by piling it high on top of rice crackers. No chopsticks needed for this finger food!

TU-NO SPREAD

1 (14-ounce [392 g]) can (1½ cups [360 g] cooked) chickpeas, drained

2 tablespoons (30 g) tahini

1 tablespoon (15 ml) rice vinegar

1 to 3 teaspoons (5 to 15 ml) sriracha

½ teaspoon onion powder

½ teaspoon salt

¼ cup (30 g) diced cucumber

¼ cup (30 g) shredded carrots

½ sheet toasted nori

TO SERVE

Sesame rice crackers

Toasted sesame seeds (optional)

1. To make the spread, in a medium bowl, combine the chickpeas, tahini, vinegar, 1 teaspoon of the sriracha, onion powder, and salt. Roughly mash with a potato masher to break down the chickpeas. Add more sriracha, to taste, depending on how spicy you'd like it.

2. Add the cucumber and carrots, mixing well to incorporate. Crumble the nori into fine flakes before adding it to the mixture. Stir to combine.

3. To serve, spoon scant tablespoons of the "tuna" mixture on top of each cracker, top with a pinch of sesame seeds, if desired, and serve immediately.

4. Stored in an airtight container in the fridge, the spicy "tuna" will keep for 5 to 7 days.

Snack Attack

chapter 3

CITRUS AND SPICE TRUFFLES

For a bite of sugar, spice, and everything nice, you can't beat these zesty chocolate morsels.

⅔ cup (80 g) Dutch process cocoa powder

⅓ cup (40 g) confectioner's sugar

½ teaspoon orange zest

½ teaspoon ground cinnamon

¼ teaspoon ground ginger

⅛ teaspoon ground cloves

⅛ teaspoon salt

¼ cup (56 g) coconut oil, melted

1. In a medium bowl, whisk together the cocoa powder, confectioner's sugar, orange zest, cinnamon, ginger, cloves, and salt.

2. Add the coconut oil and stir the mixture until it's a smooth, thick paste.

3. Carefully pour the liquid chocolate into a silicone candy mold. (Alternatively, you could use a small, lightly greased plastic container, and cut the chocolate into squares once it has set.) Place it in the fridge to set about 30 minutes.

4. Pop the chocolates out and store either at room temperature (if the room is below 75°F [24°F]) or in the refrigerator.

EDAMAME POKE

Bearing the savory flavors of garlic, soy sauce, and the bright pop of red pepper flakes melded throughout, these savory soybeans never fail to satisfy.

1 tablespoon (15 ml) olive oil

1 teaspoon toasted sesame oil

3 cloves garlic, minced

1 pound (454 g) frozen edamame in the pod

⅛ teaspoon red pepper flakes

3 tablespoons (45 ml) soy sauce

1. Combine both oils and the minced garlic in a medium sauté pan over medium heat. Cook, stirring frequently, until the garlic is aromatic but not quite browned.

2. Add the edamame (no need to thaw) along with the red pepper flakes and soy sauce, tossing to incorporate. Sauté for just about 5 minutes longer to cook and infuse the soybeans with the marinade.

3. Turn off the heat and transfer to a large serving bowl. Enjoy hot or at room temperature.

note

To make this in the microwave, simply toss everything together in a medium bowl and heat for 4 to 5 minutes total, pausing to stir every minute or so, until hot.

HOT CHOCOLATE CHIA PUDDING

Whether you serve it hot or cold, this filling cup of cocoa is a satisfying snack that comes together in mere minutes!

½ cup (120 ml) chocolate nondairy milk

2 tablespoons (16 g) chia seeds

2 tablespoons (16 g) Dutch process cocoa powder

1 tablespoon (12 g) granulated sugar

Vegan mini marshmallows, for garnish (optional)

1. Combine the milk, chia seeds, cocoa, and sugar in a small saucepan. Whisk vigorously to combine. Bring to a boil and simmer gently for 4 to 5 minutes, until thickened. (Alternatively, heat it in the microwave for 1½ minutes, letting it stand for 1 to 2 minutes to cool before removing.)

2. Top with marshmallows, if desired, and enjoy right away, or stash in the fridge until chilled.

MICROWAVE MOLTEN LAVA CAKE

No oven? No problem! You can crush chocolate cravings in mere minutes by whipping up a warm, gooey molten lava cake from scratch, right in your microwave.

¼ cup (43 g) dark chocolate chips, divided

1 tablespoon (14 g) coconut oil

1 tablespoon (12 g) granulated sugar

1½ tablespoons (12 g) all-purpose flour

1 tablespoon (8 g) Dutch process cocoa powder

1 teaspoon ground flaxseeds

¼ teaspoon baking soda

⅛ teaspoon salt

1. Lightly grease a 6-ounce (168 g) ramekin or an 8-ounce (227 g) microwave-safe mug and set aside.

2. In a small microwave-safe bowl, combine half of the chocolate chips with the coconut oil. Heat for 30 to 60 seconds, stirring vigorously until completely melted. Add the granulated sugar, mixing well.

3. In a separate bowl, whisk together the flour, cocoa powder, ground flaxseeds, baking soda, and salt. Gently fold the dry ingredients into the wet, mixing until the batter is smooth.

4. Transfer half of the mixture to your prepared ramekin or mug. Press the remainder of the chocolate chips into the center and cover with the rest of the batter.

5. Microwave on high for 1½ to 2 minutes, until set around the edges. Do not overcook! You want the center to stay gooey, and browning won't occur in the microwave.

6. Let cool for 2 minutes before turning out onto a plate or eating straight out of the ramekin or mug.

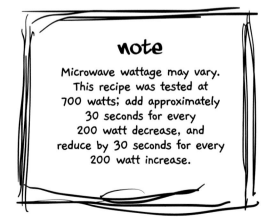

note

Microwave wattage may vary. This recipe was tested at 700 watts; add approximately 30 seconds for every 200 watt decrease, and reduce by 30 seconds for every 200 watt increase.

PEANUT SADEKO

Peanut sadeko, a Nepalese appetizer that satisfies like an entrée and tastes like a snack, combines the resounding crunch of peanuts with bold, pungent, and savory spices. Whenever the craving strikes, it hits all the right notes for instant gratification. Serve over rice, in lettuce cups, or with a spoon!

1 tablespoon (15 ml) olive oil

4 cloves garlic, minced

1 inch (2.5 cm) fresh ginger, peeled and minced, or 1¼ teaspoons ground ginger

2 cups (290 g) roasted, unsalted peanuts

1 tablespoon (15 ml) lime juice

2 Roma tomatoes, diced

1 jalapeño, thinly sliced or diced

1 teaspoon garam masala or yellow curry powder

1 teaspoon Dijon mustard

½ teaspoon salt

1 scallion, thinly sliced

½ cup (8 g) finely chopped fresh cilantro

1. Heat the oil in a medium skillet over medium heat. Once shimmering, sauté the garlic and ginger for 2 to 3 minutes, until aromatic.

2. Add the peanuts, tossing to coat and incorporate. Cook for about a minute, then drizzle with the lime juice.

3. Add the tomatoes and jalapeño, stir well, and sauté for just a minute longer, until the vegetables have softened slightly. Season with the garam masala, mustard, and salt.

4. Turn off the heat before adding the scallion and cilantro last, tossing thoroughly to blend all the ingredients evenly. Transfer to a bowl and serve.

notes

To increase the protein quotient, swap ½ cup (72 g) of the peanuts for dry-roasted edamame or chickpeas.

***

To make this in the microwave, simply combine everything except the scallion and cilantro in a large bowl. Heat for 2 to 4 minutes, stirring every minute, until the vegetables have softened and the garlic no longer tastes raw. Stir in the scallion and cilantro right before serving.

PROTEIN BARK, TWO WAYS

Just because it's technically classified as candy doesn't mean it has to be unhealthy. I'd like to think that protein bark is the new protein bar, with an extra dose of whimsy mixed in. Whether it's a gift you give to friends and family or simply to yourself, it's guaranteed to be in good taste!

PEPPERMINT CACAO BARK

6 ounces (168 g) semisweet chocolate chips

¼ cup (30 g) vegan chocolate protein powder

¼ teaspoon peppermint extract

¼ cup (30 g) cacao nibs

Coarse or flaky sea salt

CRANBERRY-PISTACHIO BARK

½ cup (112 g) coconut oil

½ cup (60 g) vegan vanilla protein powder

3 tablespoons (24 g) confectioners' sugar

¼ teaspoon vanilla bean paste or powder

¼ teaspoon salt

½ cup (73 g) toasted, unsalted pistachios

½ cup (73 g) dried cranberries

note

Store either rendition in an airtight container in the fridge or a cool place for up to a week.

For the Peppermint Cacao Bark

1. Place the chocolate chips in a microwave-safe dish and heat at 30-second intervals, stirring thoroughly between intervals, until completely melted. Add the protein powder and peppermint extract, mixing thoroughly.

2. Spread the mixture out on a piece of parchment paper or a silicone baking mat. Smooth it out as thinly as possible with a wide spatula; exact dimensions aren't important.

3. Sprinkle the cacao nibs and a pinch of sea salt over the top, gently pressing the goodies into the surface so they adhere. Place in the fridge for at least 20 minutes for the bark to solidify before breaking into pieces and enjoying.

For the Cranberry-Pistachio Bark

1. Place the coconut oil in a microwave-safe dish and heat until liquefied. Add the protein powder, confectioner's sugar, vanilla paste, and salt, stirring until the mixture is homogeneous.

2. Spread the mixture out on a piece of parchment paper or a silicone baking mat as thinly as possible with a wide spatula; exact dimensions aren't important.

3. Once smooth, sprinkle the pistachios and cranberries evenly over the top, gently pressing the goodies into the surface so they adhere. Place in the fridge for at least 20 minutes for the bark to solidify before breaking into pieces and enjoying.

PUMPKIN SPICE GUMMIES

The jubilant spirit of pumpkin spice possesses these gummy morsels with more than a merely haunting flavor. Natural sweetness rings true in each chewy bite, casting an impossibly enchanting spell.

½ cup (120 g)
pumpkin puree

1 cup (240 ml) apple juice
concentrate

1½ tablespoons (12 g)
agar powder

1 teaspoon pumpkin spice

1. Have four mini pumpkin candy molds or a comparable shape at the ready. Alternatively, you can line an 8 x 8-inch (20 x 20 cm) square baking pan with foil and plan to simply cut out gummy squares. Just be sure to lightly grease the foil before proceeding.

2. Place all the ingredients in a small saucepan over medium heat and whisk until smooth. Stir gently but consistently; you should start to feel the mixture thicken almost instantly. Continue scraping the bottom and sides of the pan as you stir to prevent sticking or burning, until the mixture is sticky but spoonable. It will be so dense that it doesn't quite come to a boil, but should bubble up around the edges quite a bit.

3. Smooth the mixture into your molds as quickly as possible, as the candy sets up very quickly. Let stand at room temperature until fully set, 20 to 30 minutes.

4. Pop the pumpkins out of the molds and trim away any excess, if necessary.

5. Store in an airtight container in the fridge for 5 to 7 days.

RASPBERRY MACAROONS

Pretty in pink, these coconut haystacks are the definition of instant gratification. Keep things exciting by changing up the jam, from strawberry to apricot, grape to blackberry, or anything else you might be able to pilfer from the dining hall.

1 cup (240 g) seedless raspberry jam

¼ cup (56 g) coconut oil, melted

1 teaspoon vanilla extract

⅛ teaspoon salt

2½ cups (200 g) unsweetened shredded coconut

1. Line a small baking sheet with parchment paper or a silicone baking mat.

2. In a medium bowl, mix together the jam, coconut oil, vanilla, and salt. Add the shredded coconut, stirring well to combine.

3. Scoop out about 1 heaping tablespoon of the mixture for each cookie, pressing firmly to make sure it sticks together. Use a small cookie scoop for greatest uniformity or use two spoons to portion out walnut-size balls. Place on the prepared baking sheet.

4. Chill until firm, at least 1 hour, or expedite the process by stashing them in the freezer for 20 minutes.

5. Store in an airtight container either in the fridge or in a cool, dark place. The cookies will keep for 5 to 7 days.

ROSEMARY TOASTED CASHEWS

When plain salted nuts and boring old trail mix just won't cut it, toss a few fresh herbs and spices into the mix to instantly jazz up your snacking routine. They're best served warm, fresh out of the skillet, but keep beautifully for days, if you can manage to keep yours hands off them that long!

2 cups (280 g) raw cashews

2 tablespoons (3 g) roughly chopped fresh rosemary or 1 tablespoon dried

2 teaspoons (10 ml) olive oil

1 teaspoon coarse salt

½ teaspoon ground black pepper

1. In a medium bowl, toss everything together to evenly coat the cashews with the seasonings.

2. Transfer to a medium skillet over medium-low heat. Cook for 5 to 6 minutes, stirring gently but continuously, until lightly golden and toasted all over.

3. Serve warm or at room temperature.

4. Store in an airtight container in a cool, dark place for 1 to 2 weeks.

notes

Feel free to use your favorite nut instead of cashews, such as almonds, pecans, walnuts, pistachios, or a blend of everything! To make this in the microwave, toss everything together in a medium microwave-safe bowl and heat for 2 to 3 minutes, stirring thoroughly every 30 to 45 seconds, until lightly golden brown.

SPECULOOS BALLS

Rum balls are a staple for holiday celebrations, but this rendition shakes things up with ground cinnamon-spike speculoos cookies, a touch of cocoa, and a creamy smear of speculoos spread—no booze necessary! The combination of warm spices and brown sugar biscuits is already intoxicating enough.

1 (7-ounce [196 g]) box speculoos cookies, finely ground into crumbs (about 1¾ cups [180 g])

1¾ cups (210 g) cashew meal or almond meal

1 cup (120 g) confectioner's sugar

¼ cup (30 g) natural cocoa powder

½ cup (120 g) smooth speculoos spread

½ cup (120 ml) apple juice

½ teaspoon rum extract (optional)

⅓ to ½ cup (40 to 60 g) pearlized silver sugar, sprinkles, or additional cookie crumbs, for rolling

1. In a large bowl, add the ground cookies, cashew meal, confectioner's sugar, and cocoa powder. Whisk to combine.

2. Add the speculoos spread, apple juice, and rum extract, if using, stirring thoroughly to incorporate. The mixture will be very thick; you may want to get in there and use your hands to make sure that there are no remaining pockets of dry ingredients.

3. Use a small cookie scoop or standard spoon to dole out tablespoon-size pieces. Roll them into balls and then toss them in the sugar, until fully coated.

4. Store in an airtight container at room temperature for about a week, or in the fridge for up to a month.

SRIRACHA KETTLE CORN

This is a delightfully fiery little snack that delivers a nice, warm burn with every bite, rounded out by a subtle touch of sweetness.

3 tablespoons (42 g) coconut oil

½ cup (110 g) popcorn kernels

⅓ cup (65 g) granulated sugar

3 to 5 teaspoons (15 to 25 ml) sriracha

½ to 1 teaspoon coarse sea salt

1. Heat the coconut oil in a large stockpot over medium heat, along with two or three kernels. Keep covered, and when the first few kernels pop, add the rest, along with the sugar and sriracha. Stir well to coat before quickly covering with the lid once more. Shake the pot constantly and vigorously to prevent your corn from burning. This is critical for even cooking and fewer "dead" (unpopped) kernels.

2. Once the popping has slowed to one every 2 to 3 seconds, remove the pot from the heat and uncover, continuing to shake for a few minutes until the popping has stopped. Pour the popcorn out onto a baking sheet and sprinkle evenly with the salt to taste. Let cool and break up the large clumps, picking through to remove any unpopped popcorn kernels that might remain.

note

To make this in the microwave, place the oil, sugar, sriracha, and salt in a large microwave-safe bowl with a vented lid. You can also cover it loosely with a slightly larger plate. Microwave until the oil is melted, about 30 seconds. Stir well to combine before adding the popcorn kernels. Cover again and microwave on high for 2 to 3 minutes. As soon as there are about 2 to 3 seconds between pops, stop cooking. Microwave times will vary and the sugar will burn quickly at the end, so err on the side of under-popping to avoid scorching your corn.

LETTUCE
CILANTRO
BELL PEPPERS
TOMATOES
AVOCADOS
CORN ON THE COB
VEGETABLE STOCK
YELLOW CORNMEAL

Eat Your Vegetables! Super Side Dishes

chapter 4

ANTS OFF A LOG SLAW

Crisp stalks of thinly sliced celery are richly coated with a sweet and spicy peanut dressing for an irresistible combination of flavors and textures. Chewy raisins and crisp, toasted nuts complete the picture, elevating the humble green vegetable into a truly craveable taste sensation.

1 pound (454 g, or 5 to 6 large stalks) celery, thinly sliced on the diagonal

1 small or ½ large tart green apple, cored and julienned

¼ cup (38 g) raisins

¼ cup (38 g) roasted, unsalted peanuts, roughly chopped

¼ cup (60 g) creamy peanut butter

3 tablespoons (45 ml) lemon juice

2 tablespoons (30 ml) soy sauce

1 clove garlic, finely minced

1 tablespoon (15 ml) water

¼ teaspoon salt

¼ teaspoon red pepper flakes

1. Place the celery, apple, raisins, and peanuts in a large bowl and toss to combine.

2. In separate bowl, whisk together the peanut butter, lemon juice, soy sauce, garlic, water, salt, and red pepper flakes until smooth.

3. Pour the dressing over the vegetables and fruits. Toss vigorously to coat.

4. Serve right away, or chill for an hour to serve cold.

note

This slaw can be stored in an airtight container in the fridge for 3 to 5 days. For best results, leave the peanuts out until just before serving to keep them crisp.

BROCCOLI CRUNCH SALAD

Crunchy, spicy, bold, and a bit brash, this raw broccoli salad is not for the meek! The contrast of sweet dates and maple syrup tames the flame for a satisfying balance of flavors and textures.

1 small crown broccoli, roughly chopped (about 4 cups)

5 pitted dates, chopped

¼ cup (38 g) toasted pepitas (hulled pumpkin seeds)

4 strips vegan bacon, cooked and chopped, ¼ cup (20 g) vegan bacon bits, or ¼ cup (28 g) chopped smoked almonds

2 scallions, thinly sliced

2 tablespoons (30 ml) olive oil

1 tablespoon (11 g) sharp English mustard

1 tablespoon (15 ml) lemon juice

2 teaspoons (10 ml) maple syrup

¼ teaspoon ground black pepper

¼ teaspoon red pepper flakes

¼ teaspoon salt

1. Combine the broccoli, dates, pepitas, bacon, and scallions in a large bowl and toss to combine.

2. In a separate bowl, combine the oil, mustard, lemon juice, maple syrup, pepper, red pepper flakes, and salt. Stir to combine.

3. Pour the dressing over the vegetables and toss to thoroughly coat.

4. Serve chilled or at room temperature.

note
The salad can be prepared up to 2 days in advance. Store in an airtight container in the fridge; leave the bacon and pepitas out until just prior to serving to keep them crisp.

CILANTRO KALE SALAD

Herbaceous cilantro vinaigrette is the ideal verdant varnish for tender leaves of kale. Crisp, tart green apple and crunchy toasted pecans provide a satisfying textural contrast, making for a simple, well-balanced side salad.

CILANTRO VINAIGRETTE

1 bunch fresh cilantro, roughly chopped

1 bunch scallions, roughly chopped

2 cloves garlic

½ cup (120 ml) olive oil

2 tablespoons (30 ml) grapefruit juice

1 tablespoon (11 g) Dijon mustard

½ teaspoon salt

¼ teaspoon ground black pepper

KALE SALAD

1 head lacinato kale, thinly sliced into ribbons

1 green apple, quartered, cored, and thinly sliced

½ cup (75 g) toasted pecans, roughly chopped

Red pepper flakes, to taste

1. To make the vinaigrette, add the ingredients to a blender or food processor and puree until smooth. Pause to scrape down the sides of the canister if needed to keep everything incorporated.

2. To make the salad, add the kale and apple to a large bowl. Add about one-third of the dressing and toss to coat. Add more dressing to taste, as desired.

3. Top with the pecans and red pepper flakes.

4. Extra dressing can be stored in an airtight container in the fridge for 5 to 7 days.

PEACH WASABI SALAD

Wasabi and peaches may sound like odd bedfellows, but once you've tried them together, the suggestion doesn't sound so unusual. Bright, assertive spice takes the lead, flaming out quickly to the round, soothing sweetness that only a truly superlative fresh peach can provide. A subtle floral quality can be found in the very best fruits, adding another dimension to this duo.

PEACH WASABI DRESSING

1 very ripe, large peach

2 tablespoons (30 g) white miso paste

½ to 1 tablespoon (7 to 14 g) wasabi paste

3 tablespoons (45 ml) lemon juice

½ cup (120 ml) olive oil

SALAD

2 to 3 Persian cucumbers or 1 English cucumber, thinly sliced

1 (10-ounce [280 g]) package (or 6 to 7 cups [300 to 350 g]) shredded cabbage or slaw mix

1 large peach, pitted and thinly sliced

½ cup (75 g) chopped, toasted pecans

1. To make the dressing, pit the peach and chop it into rough chunks. Toss it into the blender along with the miso, wasabi, and lemon juice. Blend to combine, pausing to scrape down the sides of the canister if needed to incorporate everything. With the motor running, slowly drizzle in the oil, allowing it to emulsify into a silky-smooth and thick vinaigrette. Add more wasabi to taste if desired.

2. To make the salad, in a large bowl, combine the cucumbers, cabbage, and peach. Add enough dressing to coat but not drench the mixture. Top with the chopped pecans, and serve right away.

3. Extra dressing can be stored in an airtight container in the fridge for up to 7 days.

TOTALLY RAD RADISH SALAD

With a bold dressing highlighting horseradish, this crisp salad sparkles with bright flavors. Utilizing the whole vegetable, greens and all, this raw preparation comes together very quickly, ready to start off any springtime meal on a high note.

1 bunch (about 12 ounces [340 g]) red radishes

2 to 3 Persian cucumbers

1 to 2 tablespoons (8 to 16 g) freshly grated horseradish

1 tablespoon (15 ml) red wine vinegar

1½ tablespoons (23 ml) olive oil

1 tablespoon (4 g) chopped fresh dill leaves, fronds, and/or blossoms

1 scallion, thinly sliced

Salt and ground black pepper, to taste

1. Trim off the spindly tips of the radishes and remove the greens. Rinse and reserve the leaves.

2. Thinly slice both the radishes and the cucumbers and place them in a large bowl.

3. In a separate bowl, add the horseradish, vinegar, oil, dill, scallion, and salt and pepper. Whisk to blend, breaking up the horseradish so that it's not clumped into one bite. Adjust the seasonings to taste.

4. Pour the dressing over the sliced cucumbers and radishes, tossing thoroughly to evenly coat the vegetables.

5. Arrange the reserved leafy greens on salad plates and top with the dressed veggies. Serve immediately.

SUCCOTASH SALAD

Pared down to the essentials, succotash is a celebration of summer vegetables at the peak of perfection. Switch it up by adding diced bell peppers, either raw or roasted, sliced fresh okra, or lightly sautéed zucchini. Serve over leafy greens to make it a more conventional starter salad or bulk it up with additional beans to enjoy as an entrée.

1 cup (240 g) baby lima beans, fresh or frozen, cooked until al dente

3 cups (450 g) corn kernels, fresh, frozen, or canned and drained

1 pint (300 g) cherry or grape tomatoes, halved

1 tablespoon (15 ml) red wine vinegar

1 tablespoon (15 ml) olive oil

¼ cup (16 g) minced fresh parsley or (4 g) cilantro

2 scallions, thinly sliced

½ teaspoon salt

¼ teaspoon ground black pepper

1. This is a complicated procedure, so prepare yourself. Mix everything together in a large bowl, tossing to thoroughly combine.

2. Serve right away at room temperature or refrigerate for up to 3 days and serve chilled. That's all, folks.

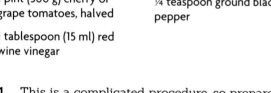
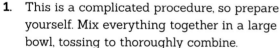

notes

Raw lima beans can be unpleasantly starchy. Either lightly steam them in the microwave for 2 to 3 minutes, blanch in boiling water for 1 to 2 minutes, or sauté with a drizzle of olive oil for 2 to 3 minutes for the best flavor.

If you're not a fan of lima beans, you can use an equal amount of shelled edamame instead.

SUNSHINE SALAD

Ready, set, glow! Bathed in a golden peanut dressing, sunflower sprouts and seeds mix with shaved gold beets, shredded carrots, and edamame.

GOLDEN PEANUT DRESSING

¼ cup (60 g) creamy peanut butter

3 tablespoons (45 ml) lemon juice

1 teaspoon ground turmeric

½ teaspoon garlic powder

⅛ teaspoon cayenne pepper

¼ teaspoon salt

SALAD

1 head green or red leaf lettuce, roughly chopped

3 cups (90 g) sunflower sprouts

1 cup (120 g) shredded carrots

1 medium gold beet, peeled, halved, and very thinly sliced

½ cup (100 g) shelled edamame

¼ cup (35 g) toasted, unsalted sunflower seeds

1. To make the dressing, whisk all the ingredients together in a small bowl until smooth, slowly drizzling in a little extra water, if needed, to reach your desired consistency.

2. To make the salad, combine the lettuce, sprouts, shredded carrots, beets, edamame, and sunflower seeds in a large bowl. Serve with dressing on the side, or drizzle generously and toss to coat.

note

If sunflower sprouts are unavailable, substitute pea shoots, watercress, or baby arugula.

DIRTY CAULIFLOWER RICE

This recipe is a fully plant-based take on a Creole classic. The only meat you'll find in this modern revamp is in the form of nutmeat. Minced walnuts add a hearty dose of protein and richness, complementing a bold palate of spices. Cauliflower stands in for rice, further lightening the dish. Filled with aromatics and herbs like onion, pepper, celery, garlic, chili powder, paprika, and thyme, this savory, flavor-filled dish makes a great healthy side for stewed black beans or grilled vegan sausage.

2 tablespoons (30 ml) olive oil

1 small red onion, diced

½ green bell pepper, diced

2 stalks celery, diced

2 cloves garlic, minced

1 teaspoon chili powder

1 teaspoon smoked paprika

1 teaspoon dried thyme

1 pound (454 g) riced cauliflower

1 tablespoon (15 ml) soy sauce

1 cup (150 g) minced, toasted walnuts

½ teaspoon salt

½ teaspoon ground black pepper

2 scallions, thinly sliced (optional)

1. Heat the oil in a skillet over medium heat. Add the onion, bell pepper, and celery, and sauté until lightly browned, 6 to 7 minutes.

2. Add the garlic and continue cooking until the whole mixture is highly aromatic, another 5 minutes.

3. Sprinkle in the chili powder, paprika, and thyme; add the riced cauliflower and stir.

4. Drizzle with the soy sauce, scraping the bottom of the pan thoroughly with your spatula to make sure all those delicious caramelized vegetables are incorporated. Cook until the cauliflower is tender, 5 to 8 minutes longer.

5. Stir in the chopped walnuts; season with salt and pepper. Top with the scallions, if using, and serve immediately.

note

Don't have all of the spices on hand? Pick up a Creole spice blend and use instead of the chili powder, paprika, and thyme. The cauliflower rice is best consumed the day it is made, but you can reheat leftovers the next day with red beans for a savory breakfast or lunch.

SAUERKRAUT COLCANNON

Lacking fresh cabbage when a sudden craving hit, I smashed some pleasantly tangy, satisfyingly salty sauerkraut into mashed potatoes for an upgraded, invigorating take on Irish colcannon.

1 pound (454 g) Yukon gold potatoes, roughly diced

3 tablespoons (45 ml) olive oil, divided

½ medium yellow onion, diced

1 clove garlic, minced

1 cup (240 g) sauerkraut, drained

⅔ cup (160 ml) unsweetened nondairy milk

¼ teaspoon salt

¼ teaspoon ground black pepper

Fresh parsley, minced (optional)

note

To make this in the microwave, place the diced potatoes, 2 tablespoons of oil, onion, and garlic in a medium bowl and cover loosely with a lid or slightly larger plate. Heat for 8 to 12 minutes, until fork-tender. Add the sauerkraut and nondairy milk, and heat for an additional 2 to 3 minutes. Mash roughly and season with the salt, pepper, and parsley, if using. Top with the remaining 1 tablespoon (15 ml) oil and serve piping hot.

1. Place the potatoes in a small saucepan and cover with water. Bring to a boil over medium heat, then reduce the heat and simmer until the pieces are fork-tender; 10 to 15 minutes. Drain thoroughly.

2. Meanwhile, in a medium saucepan over medium heat, warm 2 tablespoons (30 ml) of the oil. Add the onion and garlic, and sauté until softened and aromatic, 6 to 8 minutes.

3. Add the sauerkraut and cook, stirring frequently, for 3 more minutes. Add the nondairy milk and bring to a simmer.

4. Add the cooked potatoes, salt, pepper, and parsley, if using. Roughly mash to your desired consistency.

5. Transfer to a bowl and top with the remaining 1 tablespoon (15 ml) olive oil. Enjoy right away!

STIR-FRIED TAIWANESE CABBAGE

Here is cabbage like you've never tasted before: tender, rich, and almost buttery. This quick stir-fry will change the way you think about the humble green leaves.

1 tablespoon (15 ml) olive oil

2 cloves garlic, minced

1 pound (454 g) Taiwanese or green cabbage, sliced into ½-inch (1.3 cm)-wide ribbons

1 tablespoon (15 ml) soy sauce

1 tablespoon (15 ml) rice wine vinegar

1 teaspoon granulated sugar

½ teaspoon red pepper flakes (optional)

¼ teaspoon salt

1. Heat the oil in a large skillet over medium heat. Add the garlic and cook for a few seconds until aromatic and lightly browned.

2. Stir in the cabbage until all the pieces are thoroughly coated in the oil, then cover the pan. Let cook, undisturbed, for 1 minute.

3. Sprinkle with the soy sauce, vinegar, sugar, red pepper flakes (if using), and salt all at once, increasing the heat to high, and cook until the cabbage is tender, 2 to 4 minutes. Serve immediately.

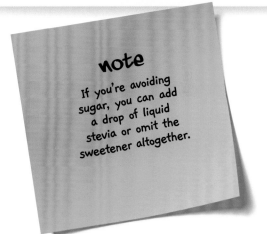

note

If you're avoiding sugar, you can add a drop of liquid stevia or omit the sweetener altogether.

SWEET POTATO HALUSKI

Call me a rabbit, but I happen to love cabbage. No shame, no judgment, please. Simmered until it practically melts in your mouth, cabbage has a silky texture that I crave more than some people crave the crunch of potato chips.

Focusing on the vegetables and getting straight to the good stuff, I decided to put an entirely plant-based spin on Russian haluski, in the truest sense of the concept. Swapping out wheat noodles for potato ribbons, this one comes together in a snap, with fewer calories, more fiber, and ever greater flavor.

2 tablespoons (28 g) vegan butter or olive oil

1 medium yellow onion, quartered and thinly sliced

1 pound (454 g, or ½ medium) green cabbage, roughly chopped

4 cloves garlic, minced

½ teaspoon salt

⅛ teaspoon baking soda

1 tablespoon (15 ml) sherry vinegar

¼ to ½ cup (60 to 120 ml) vegetable stock

8 ounces (227 g, or 1 large) white sweet potato, peeled and shaved into thin ribbons

2 tablespoons (8 g) finely minced fresh dill

1. Heat the butter in a large saucepan over medium heat. Add the onion, cabbage, garlic, and salt. Cook, stirring occasionally, for 5 minutes, or until softened.

2. Sprinkle in the baking soda and mix thoroughly to incorporate. Sauté for 10 to 15 minutes longer, adding the vinegar and the vegetable stock, just 1 to 2 tablespoons (15 to 30) at a time, to prevent the vegetables from sticking and burning. The mixture should be golden brown and very tender.

3. Add the sweet potato ribbons and use a wide spatula to gentle fold them into the mixture. Cook for just 1 to 2 minutes longer, until the ribbons have softened and are pliable like noodles.

4. Remove from the heat, top with the dill, and serve hot.

note

You can use a standard sweet potato or yam with orange flesh as well; it just won't look quite as convincingly like conventional ribbon noodles.

WINTER TABBOULEH

Even the longest winter can feel far more manageable with a good supply of fresh, simple recipes on hand. Replace the traditional tomatoes with persimmons in this Middle Eastern composition for a refreshing change of pace when produce is scarce. Their juicy, meaty texture and natural sweetness completely transform the dish into a brand-new celebration of the colder seasons.

¼ cup (48 g) dried bulgur wheat

¼ teaspoon ground turmeric

½ cup (120 ml) vegetable stock

1 Fuyu persimmon, peeled, stemmed, and chopped

⅓ cup (40 g) pomegranate arils (optional)

1½ cups (96 g) minced carrot top fronds

1 cup (60 g) minced fresh parsley

2 tablespoons (20 g) finely chopped red onion

2 to 3 tablespoons (30 to 45 ml) lemon juice

2 to 3 tablespoons (30 to 45 ml) olive oil

Salt and ground black pepper, to taste

1. In a small saucepan, combine the bulgur wheat, turmeric, and vegetable stock, and place over low heat. Stir well and bring to a boil. Cover, turn off the heat, and let stand for 15 to 20 minutes, until all of the liquid has been absorbed. Let cool slightly.

2. Meanwhile, in a large bowl, combine the persimmon, pomegranate arils, carrot fronds, parsley, and onion. Add the cooled bulgur and stir to combine.

3. In a small bowl, combine the lemon juice, olive oil, and salt and pepper, adjusting the seasonings to taste. Pour over the bulgur and toss to coat.

4. Cover and chill for at least 2 hours before serving to allow the flavors to marry.

note

To make this in the microwave, simply heat the bulgur, turmeric, and stock in a large bowl for 3 minutes, or until the liquid comes to a boil. Cover with a lid or slightly larger plate, and proceed with the recipe as written.

LETTUCE
CILANTRO
BELL PEPPERS
TOMATOES
AVOCADOS
CORN ON THE COB
VEGETABLE STOCK
YELLOW CORNMEAL

Noodling Around

chapter 5

CREAMY GREEN PESTO PASTA

Gotta get those greens in, even during the stress of final exams! Fresh, frozen, or even powdered, this vibrant pesto sauce makes it easy being green anytime.

1 tablespoon (15 ml) olive oil

4 cloves garlic, minced

4 to 5 cups (280 to 350 g) chopped kale, spinach, and/or arugula, or 4 to 5 tablespoons (32 to 40 g) powdered greens

1 (15-ounce [420 g]) can full-fat coconut milk

¼ cup (10 g) packed chopped fresh basil

¼ cup (25 g) chopped scallion or 1 teaspoon onion powder

2 teaspoons (10 ml) lemon juice

2 cups (300 g) frozen green peas, thawed

1 pound (454 g) pasta, cooked

Salt and ground black pepper, to taste

1. Heat the oil in a small skillet over medium heat. Add the garlic and cook until fragrant and lightly golden, 1 to 2 minutes. If using fresh greens, add them and cook for another 3 to 4 minutes, until wilted down. Transfer to your blender or food processor.

2. If using powdered greens, add it to the blender now, along with the coconut milk, basil, scallion, and lemon juice. Puree until smooth.

3. Place the peas and pasta in a large bowl. Add the pesto mixture and toss to coat, seasoning to taste with salt and pepper.

4. Serve warm, or chill for at least an hour to serve as a cold pasta salad. Keep in an airtight container in the refrigerator for up to 5 days.

ELOTE PASTA SALAD

On or off the cob, Mexican street corn is a simple snack that celebrates the golden kernels with a cloak of creamy, cheesy, and subtly spiced sauce. Add some pasta to extend those fresh flavors and make it a more substantial dish.

CREMA DRESSING

¾ cup (180 g) vegan mayonnaise

2 tablespoons (12 g) nutritional yeast

2 tablespoons (30 ml) lime juice

¼ cup (60 ml) water

½ teaspoon smoked paprika

½ teaspoon garlic powder

1 teaspoon salt

ELOTE PASTA SALAD

8 ounces (227 g) rotini pasta

2 cups (300 g) corn kernels, canned and drained or frozen and thawed

1 roasted red pepper, diced

1 cup (150 g) halved cherry or grape tomatoes

1 cup (116 g) diced jicama or radishes

1 avocado, peeled, pitted, and diced

¼ cup (4 g) chopped cilantro

2 scallions, thinly sliced

½ jalapeño, minced (optional)

1. To make the crema dressing, combine all the ingredients in a medium bowl and whisk vigorously until completely smooth. Set aside.

2. To make the pasta salad, fill a large pot with well-salted water and bring to a boil over high heat. Cook the pasta according to package directions. Strain, rinse with cold water until completely cool, and thoroughly drain. Place in a large bowl.

3. Add the corn, red pepper, tomatoes, jicama, avocado, cilantro, scallions, and jalapeño (if using). Add the dressing and toss to combine.

4. Serve immediately, or store in an airtight container in the fridge for 3 to 5 days.

KASHA TWISTS

Departing slightly from the traditional path of kasha varnishkes, I'm *twisting* up the pasta shape because *varnishkes* translates to "bow-tie pasta" in Yiddish. The secret to savory success for this one is using lots of onions and plenty of vegan butter. You could fancy it up and add mushrooms, Brussels sprouts, and/or chickpeas, but it's a perfectly comforting dish when it's kept plain and simple.

1 cup (170 g) toasted buckwheat

2 cups (480 ml) mushroom or vegetable stock

½ cup (112 g) vegan butter

1 large yellow onion, diced

1 clove garlic, minced

½ teaspoon salt

¼ teaspoon ground black pepper

12 ounces (340 g) pasta twists, cooked al dente

2 scallions, thinly sliced

2 tablespoons (8 g) minced fresh parsley

1. Combine the buckwheat and stock in a medium saucepan over medium heat. Bring to a boil, cover, and reduce the heat to low. Gently simmer for 10 to 15 minutes, until the liquid is mostly absorbed. Turn off the heat and let sit for 10 minutes. Fluff with a fork.

2. Meanwhile, melt the butter in a medium sauté pan over medium heat. Add the onion and garlic, and cook until golden brown and highly aromatic, 10 to 15 minutes. Season with the salt and pepper.

3. In a large bowl, combine the cooked buckwheat, buttery onions, and cooked pasta. Add the scallions and parsley and toss to combine. Enjoy hot.

Amazing

NO-MATO MEATLESS BOLOGNESE

No nightshades needed with this rich sauce, which sings of highly aromatic herbs and savory seasonings. Beets and carrots build a solid foundation that can support any noodle in need, be it wheat, bean-based, zucchini, or more. Omit the nuts for a simple marinara, puree to slather it on pizza, layer it in for lasagna, add extra juice to soup it up, or add a splash of coconut milk for a creamier concoction.

1 tablespoon (15 ml) olive oil

1 large red onion, finely diced

4 cloves garlic, minced

6 medium carrots, peeled and finely diced

2 medium red beets, peeled and finely diced

2 stalks celery, finely diced

¼ cup (45 g) dried red lentils

1 dried bay leaf

1½ to 2 cups (360 to 480 ml) beet juice

1 cup (150 g) raw pecans or walnuts, roughly chopped

1 tablespoon (6 g) nutritional yeast

1 teaspoon dried oregano

½ to ¾ teaspoon salt

1 tablespoon (2.5 g) minced fresh basil

1 pound (454 g) spiralized zucchini or spaghetti, cooked al dente

1. Heat the oil in a medium saucepan over medium heat. Add the onion and garlic, and sauté for about 10 minutes, until aromatic and golden all over. Add the carrots, beet, and celery, and cook for 2 minutes longer.

2. Add the lentils, bay leaf, and 1½ cups of juice. Cover, lower the heat to a gentle simmer, and cook for about 30 minutes, or until the vegetables are very tender.

3. If you'd like a smoother texture, transfer half or all of the vegetables to a blender and puree. Pour back into the saucepan and stir well.

4. Add the nuts, nutritional yeast, oregano, and ½ teaspoon of salt. Simmer for another 10 minutes. Adjust the consistency by adding more juice if desired, and if needed, season with more salt to taste. Turn off the heat and add the basil.

5. Serve hot over spiralized zucchini.

6. Once cooled to room temperature, leftover sauce can be stored in an airtight container in the fridge for up to a week, or in the freezer for up to 4 months.

PENNE ALLA ROSA

Smooth, with a few chunks of diced tomatoes for a more satisfying texture, this rosy pink pasta sauce is enriched with coconut milk rather than traditional heavy cream.

½ cup (112 g) coconut oil

1 large onion, finely minced

1 cup (240 ml) vegetable stock

2 (28-ounce [784 g]) cans diced tomatoes

1 (14-ounce [392 g]) can full-fat coconut milk

Salt and ground black pepper, to taste

1 pound (454 g) penne pasta, cooked al dente

note

To prepare the sauce in advance, cool completely before storing in an airtight container in the fridge for up to 1 week.

1. Melt the coconut oil in a large saucepan over medium heat, add the onion, and sauté until softened and just beginning to take on a brown color, 5 to 7 minutes.

2. Add the stock and stir well, scraping up all the brown bits from the bottom of the pan, and cook for 10 minutes.

3. Add the canned tomatoes, juice and all, and bring the mixture up to a rapid bubble. Reduce the heat to medium-low to keep the sauce at a steady, low simmer, and cook for another 30 minutes.

4. Add the coconut milk and cook for 30 minutes longer. Season to taste with salt and pepper, being generous with both.

5. Transfer half of the sauce to a blender and puree or use an immersion blender until it reaches your desired consistency. Be sure to leave it slightly chunky.

6. Place the cooked pasta in a bowl, add the sauce, and toss to coat. Serve hot.

SPAGHETTI ABCDEFGHIJK-O'S

No matter how old you get, you never outgrow certain nostalgic comfort foods, even if they're just canned pasta rings in tomato sauce. It's hard to hunt down plain O's to start from scratch, but the full alphabet is readily available in most stores. Failing that, regular old orzo or Israeli couscous will be less verbose, but equally delicious.

1 (15-ounce [420 g]) can tomato sauce

¼ cup (56 g) vegan butter

¼ cup (24 g) nutritional yeast

1½ teaspoons soy sauce

1 teaspoon granulated sugar

1 teaspoon onion powder

½ teaspoon garlic powder

¼ teaspoon salt

7 ounces (196 g) alphabet pasta, cooked al dente

1. Add the tomato sauce and butter to a medium saucepan over medium heat. Stir periodically until the butter has melted. Add the nutritional yeast, soy sauce, sugar, onion powder, garlic powder, and salt. Bring to a simmer and turn off the heat.

2. Toss in the cooked pasta and stir well to incorporate. Serve hot.

note

If you're avoiding sugar, you can add either a drop of liquid stevia or omit the sweetener altogether.

SIMPLE SINGAPORE NOODLES

I'm forever trying to reduce the number of pans, bowls, spoons, and spatulas I need to scrub at the end of the day, so one-pan meals are my jam. It's all about building layers of flavor, adding ingredients strategically so everything is done cooking at the same time. Turns out Singapore noodles, tinged with golden curry powder and tangled up with any assortment of vegetables, lend themselves perfectly to the format.

2 tablespoons (30 ml) olive oil

3 cloves garlic, minced

1 inch (2.5 cm) fresh ginger, peeled and minced

8 ounces (227 g) vegan shrimp, cubed extra-firm tofu, or sliced tempeh

1 (12-ounce [340 g]) bag frozen stir-fry vegetables

1 tablespoon (15 ml) soy sauce

1 tablespoon (8 g) yellow curry powder

1 teaspoon firmly packed dark brown sugar

4 cups (960 ml) vegetable stock

8 ounces (227 g) rice vermicelli noodles

2 scallions, thinly sliced

1. Heat the oil in a pan over medium heat. Once shimmering, add the garlic and ginger, and sauté until aromatic, 3 to 4 minutes. Add the vegan shrimp and frozen vegetables (no need to thaw) and cook for another 5 to 8 minutes, until vibrant and tender.

2. Mix in the soy sauce, curry powder, brown sugar, and vegetable stock. Break the vermicelli in half to fit, pressing it down so it's covered by the liquid.

3. Cover with the lid and bring to a gentle simmer. Stir well and cook for about 10 minutes. The liquid should be mostly absorbed by the noodles at this point. Let sit, uncovered, for another minute or two to fully hydrate.

4. Add the scallions, toss to combine, and serve right away.

STOVE TOP MAC & CHEESE

Make your own velvety cheese sauce that's even better than the boxed stuff, without any dairy. Is this the best mac and cheese recipe on earth? I'm not saying that . . . but you just might.

½ cup (70 g) peeled and diced Yukon gold potatoes

⅓ cup (50 g) raw cashews

¼ cup (45 g) dried red lentils

¼ cup (30 g) shredded carrots

½ cup (80 g) chopped yellow onion

1 clove garlic, thinly sliced

1¼ cups (300 ml) vegetable stock

¼ cup (24 g) nutritional yeast

2 tablespoons (30 g) white miso paste

1 tablespoon (15 ml) rice vinegar

½ teaspoon Dijon mustard

½ teaspoon salt

¼ teaspoon smoked paprika

⅛ teaspoon turmeric (optional, for color)

1 cup (240 ml) unsweetened, plain nondairy milk

½ cup (112 g) vegan butter, melted

1 pound (454 g) pasta, cooked al dente

1. In a small saucepan, combine the potatoes, cashews, lentils, carrot, onion, garlic, and stock. Set over medium heat and bring to a boil.

2. Once the water reaches a vigorous boil, cover the pot, turn down the heat to medium-low, and let simmer for 15 minutes, until the lentils are cooked through and the potatoes are extremely tender.

3. Meanwhile, place the nutritional yeast, miso, vinegar, mustard, salt, paprika, and turmeric (if using) in a blender. When the vegetables on the stove are fully cooked and ready, pour them into the blender along with any excess stock. Add the nondairy milk and turn on the blender to its highest setting. Thoroughly puree the mixture until completely smooth and lump-free. If you're using a blender that isn't so powerful, this could take 6 to 10 minutes.

4. With the motor still running, slowly drizzle in the melted butter, allowing it to properly emulsify.

5. Place the cooked noodles in a large bowl, add the sauce, toss to combine, and serve immediately.

SWEET & SPICY CHILLED ALMOND NOODLES

When it's too hot outside to stand in front of the stove all day, don't lose your cool. Cook a big batch of food once, early in the day, and enjoy it chilled later. That's the theory behind pasta salad, which is also wonderful because you can throw pretty much any scraps into it for a different spin every time. If you want a completely heat-free option, you could always toss it with fresh zucchini noodles instead.

ALMOND SAUCE

½ cup (120 g) creamy almond butter

¼ cup (60 ml) soy sauce

2 tablespoons (30 ml) rice vinegar

1 tablespoon (15 ml) toasted sesame oil

1 teaspoon ground ginger

1 clove garlic, minced

1 teaspoon sriracha

¼ cup (60 ml) water

PASTA SALAD

1 pound (454 g) spaghetti or linguine, cooked al dente

1 red bell pepper, seeded and sliced

1 yellow bell pepper, seeded and sliced

1 green bell pepper, seeded and sliced

2 cups (60 g) baby arugula

Salt and ground black pepper, to taste

½ cup (55 g) sliced almonds

¼ cup (4 g) minced fresh cilantro

1. To make the sauce, in a large bowl, combine all the ingredients and whisk until smooth.

2. To make the pasta salad, add the pasta, peppers, and arugula to the bowl with the sauce, tossing to coat. Season with salt and pepper.

3. Transfer to a serving dish and top with the sliced almonds and cilantro. Chill until ready to eat.

note

You may need to add a bit more water if the salad sits for a while in the fridge, since the pasta absorbs a bit; adjust as needed.

Soup's On
chapter 6

ALL-SEASONS BORSCHT

Call me an eighty-year-old bubbeh at heart, but I love this old-world stew. Best of all, you can serve it hot or chilled with equal success, so it's perfect for unpredictable weather.

2 tablespoons (30 ml) olive oil

1 medium leek, cleaned and sliced

4 cloves garlic, minced

2 stalks celery, diced

1 carrot, peeled and diced

2 medium red beets, peeled and diced

1 medium turnip, peeled and diced

2 tablespoons (30 g) tomato paste

½ teaspoon smoked paprika

¼ teaspoon dried thyme

4 cups (960 ml) vegetable stock

2 tablespoons (30 ml) apple cider vinegar

1 tablespoon (15 ml) soy sauce

¼ teaspoon salt

¼ teaspoon ground black pepper

½ cup (58 g) thinly sliced radishes

2 tablespoons (8 g) minced fresh dill

1. Heat the oil in a large stockpot over medium heat, then add the leek, garlic, celery, and carrot. Sauté for about 5 to 6 minutes, until the vegetables are softened and aromatic.

2. Add the beets, turnip, tomato paste, smoked paprika, thyme, vegetable stock, vinegar, and soy sauce. Cover and bring to a boil, then reduce the heat to medium-low. Simmer for 20 to 30 minutes, until the beets are fork-tender. Season with the salt and pepper.

3. Ladle into bowls and top each serving with the sliced radishes and fresh dill. Enjoy hot, or chill for at least an hour to enjoy cold.

BUFFALO RANCH CHICKPEA STEW

Simple and easy enough to suit the most hectic weekday dinner rush, this hearty stew combines the best parts of a Buffalo wing marinade with a few pantry staples, elevating it well beyond standard bar fare. Thick and rich, each spoonful sparkles with just the right spice to ring true. Who needs fried fast food when little more than a few humble beans can trump the whole flavor sensation? A cooling ranch crème balances out the heat, and of course, a generous handful of crunchy ranch chickpeas adds some textural contrast to complete the picture.

BUFFALO CHICKPEA STEW

2 tablespoons (30 ml) olive oil

½ large yellow onion, diced

2 cloves garlic, minced

3 stalks celery, diced

3 tablespoons (24 g) chickpea flour

1 cup (240 ml) low-sodium vegetable broth

½ cup (120 ml) tomato puree

1 (14-ounce [392 g]) can (1¾ cups [360 g] cooked) chickpeas, drained

2 tablespoons (30 ml) hot sauce

Salt, to taste

RANCH CRÈME

½ cup (120 g) vegan sour cream

1 teaspoon apple cider vinegar

2 tablespoons (8 g) finely minced fresh parsley

½ teaspoon garlic powder

½ teaspoon onion powder

½ teaspoon salt

¼ teaspoon ground black pepper

TO SERVE (OPTIONAL)

Ranch-flavored crunchy chickpeas

1 to 2 scallions, thinly sliced

1. To make the stew, heat the oil in a medium pot over medium heat. Add the onion, garlic, and celery, and sauté until softened, aromatic, and just beginning to caramelize around the edges.

2. Sprinkle in the chickpea flour and stir well, coating the vegetables. Cook lightly, for just a minute or two, to gently toast and cook the raw flavor out of the flour. Slowly add the vegetable broth, stirring constantly to ensure that it properly hydrates the flour without clumping. Bring to a simmer.

3. Add the tomato puree, chickpeas, and hot sauce, stirring well. Turn the heat down to medium-low and let simmer until the liquid has significantly thickened, 10 to 15 minutes. Season with salt.

4. Meanwhile, to make the ranch crème, combine all the ingredients in a small bowl and whisk to blend. Keep refrigerated until ready to serve.

5. To serve, ladle the stew into individual serving bowls. Top with dollops of the ranch crème and the chickpeas and scallions, if using.

CREAMY CHICKEN RAMEN

Be it an emotional malaise or a physical flu, this soup will cure what ails you, or at least provide a serious serving of comfort through it all. Such simple flavors are universally appealing; it's the ramen that could very well unite a nation.

3 ounces (84 g) dry ramen noodles (straight or curly)

½ cup (120 ml) unsweetened nondairy milk

½ cup (120 ml) water

2 teaspoons (6 g) tapioca starch or cornstarch

1 teaspoon no-chicken broth powder or paste

1 teaspoon soy sauce

1½ teaspoons vegan butter

Thinly sliced scallions, for serving (optional)

1. Bring a small pot of water to a boil and cook the noodles to al dente, as directed on the package. Drain thoroughly and place in a bowl.

2. Meanwhile, in a small saucepan, combine the nondairy milk, water, starch, broth powder, and soy sauce over medium-low heat. Stir vigorously to ensure there are no clumps of starch. Cook until thickened and bubbles break with regularity on the surface, about 5 minutes. Turn off the heat, add the vegan butter, and stir until melted and smoothly incorporated.

3. Add the sauce to the noodles, toss to coat, and top with the scallions, if desired. Slurp away without delay!

note

Run out of ramen? You can use spaghetti! It won't be quite the same experience, but you can approximate the texture of ramen noodles by boiling the spaghetti in a quart of water mixed with 2 teaspoons (6 g) of baking soda. This alkalizes the noodles, making them chewier and brighter yellow, too.

HEAT 'N EAT CREAMY TOMATO BISQUE

Whole cashews are cooked right into the mix for this almost instant blend, transforming humble broth and vegetables into an impossibly luscious, creamy bisque. Fire-roasted and sun-dried tomatoes join forces to lend a robust, full-bodied tomato flavor that tastes like it spent all day simmering on the stove.

1 tablespoon (15 ml) olive oil

1 medium yellow onion, diced

3 cloves garlic, minced

1 teaspoon salt

4 cups (960 ml) low-sodium vegetable stock

1 (28-ounce [784 g]) can fire-roasted crushed tomatoes

½ cup (50 g) sun-dried tomatoes

½ cup (75g) raw cashews or slivered almonds

2 tablespoons (12 g) nutritional yeast

1 tablespoon (15 ml) balsamic vinegar

½ teaspoon ground black pepper

½ cup (15 g) julienned (thinly sliced) fresh basil

1. Heat the oil in a large saucepan over medium heat. Add the onion and garlic, and cook until softened, about 5 minutes. Sprinkle in the salt and continuing cooking for about 10 minutes, until the onions begin to brown. Be patient while caramelizing the onions because the more deeply golden-brown they get, the more flavorful your soup will be.

2. Add the vegetable stock, undrained can of tomatoes, sun-dried tomatoes, cashews, nutritional yeast, vinegar, and black pepper. Cover and bring to a boil.

3. Reduce the heat and simmer for 25 to 30 minutes, until the cashews are soft and the liquid has slightly reduced.

4. Transfer the soup to a blender and thoroughly puree until completely smooth.

5. Ladle into bowls and garnish with the basil.

CRAZY GOOD COCONUT CORN CHOWDER

Creamy, comforting soup meets the dazzling flavor of fresh summer corn in this hearty blend. Subtle, natural sweetness rounds out each spoonful thanks to the richness of coconut milk. Though best when made with peak-season produce, frozen and thawed corn can be substituted in a pinch.

2 tablespoons (30 ml) olive oil

1 small sweet onion, diced

2 stalks celery, diced

2 cloves garlic, minced

½ teaspoon dried thyme

½ teaspoon smoked paprika

¼ cup (30 g) all-purpose flour

4 cups (960 ml) vegetable stock, divided

1 (14-ounce [392 g]) can coconut milk

2 medium sweet potatoes, peeled and diced

4 cups (600 g) fresh sweet corn kernels (from about 8 ears)

½ teaspoon salt

¼ teaspoon ground black pepper

3 tablespoons (9 g) thinly sliced chives

1. Heat the olive oil in large pot over medium heat. Add the onion, celery, and garlic, and sauté until the vegetables are lightly browned and highly aromatic, 8 to 10 minutes. Sprinkle the thyme, paprika, and flour over the mixture, coating all the vegetables evenly.

2. Slowly pour in 1 cup (240 ml) of the vegetable stock, stirring to incorporate the flour smoothly. Let simmer until thickened, 3 to 4 minutes, then gradually add the remaining 3 cups (720 ml) stock and the coconut milk. This process will help prevent any clumps of flour from forming.

3. Add the sweet potatoes, corn, salt, and pepper, cover, and bring to a full boil. Reduce the heat to a simmer and cook until the sweet potatoes are fork-tender, about 15 minutes.

4. Transfer half of the soup to a blender or food processor and puree until silky smooth. Pour the creamy blend back into the pot, stirring well. Feel free to blend more or less depending on how creamy or chunky you prefer your chowder.

5. Ladle the hot soup into bowls and top with the chives.

GOLDEN ONION SOUP

In an Ayurvedic twist inspired by sweet golden milk, this soup glows with gilded turmeric and ginger-laced broth. Creamy coconut milk swirls throughout, lending body to this soulful bowlful, ensuring a satisfying experience down to the last spoonful.

¼ cup (56 g) vegan butter or coconut oil

4 sweet Vidalia onions, quartered and thinly sliced

2 cloves garlic, minced

½ inch (1.3 cm) fresh ginger, peeled and minced

½ teaspoon salt

2 tablespoons (16 g) chickpea flour

1 teaspoon ground turmeric

½ cup (120 ml) full-fat coconut milk

2 tablespoons (30 g) white miso paste

4 to 5 cups (960 to 1200 ml) vegetable stock

½ teaspoon ground black pepper

¼ teaspoon cayenne pepper

1. In a large stockpot, melt the butter or coconut oil over medium heat. Add the onions and cook, stirring frequently, for about 30 minutes, or until lightly caramelized and highly aromatic.

2. Add the garlic, ginger, and salt, and sauté for 30 minutes longer, stirring every 5 minutes. The mixture should be very soft and amber brown.

3. Add the flour and turmeric, stirring to incorporate. Sauté for 2 to 3 minutes to lightly toast the flour. Add the coconut milk and use a wooden spoon to scrape the bottom of the pan to incorporate all the brown bits.

4. In a medium bowl, combine the miso paste and stock, whisking until fully dissolved. Add to the stockpot and stir to combine. Bring the soup to a simmer, reduce the heat to medium-low, and simmer gently for 15 to 20 minutes.

5. Season with the black and cayenne pepper and add more stock or water, if needed, to reach your desired thickness.

FRESH PEA SOUP

This simple, fresh pea soup draws out the bright, green flavor from each tender sphere and allows them to shine.

1 tablespoon (15 ml) olive oil

1 large yellow onion, diced

2 to 3 cups (480 to 720 ml) vegetable stock

1 pound (454 g) fresh or frozen and thawed green peas, plus more for garnish

Salt, to taste

Pea shoots, for garnish (optional)

1. Heat the oil in a large stockpot over medium-low heat. Add the onions and sauté for 4 to 5 minutes, stirring well to coat with the oil. Add 2 cups of the stock, cover, and cook for about 20 minutes. You don't want the onions to brown or caramelize at all, but cook down practically to mush.

2. Rinse the peas under hot water, add them to the pot, and cook gently for 5 to 10 minutes until tender, if using fresh. For frozen peas, immediately turn off the heat and don't let them cook much at all. You want to preserve that brilliant green color, and they've already been blanched prior to freezing so they're precooked.

3. Transfer the mixture to a blender and puree, adding more broth if desired, until the soup reaches your desired consistency. You may need to do this in batches, depending on the capacity of your blender. Add a pinch of salt and blend well.

4. Ladle into bowls and top with additional peas and/or pea shoots, if desired.

just like Mom's

INSTANT FIESTA SOUP

If you can open a can and operate a microwave, you can feed yourself very well indeed. The beauty of this formula is that it's infinitely adaptable to any type of beans or seasoning you can scrounge up. See the variations for more inspiration, but don't be afraid to depart from the beaten path; embark on a new flavor adventure.

SOUP

2 (15-ounce [420 g]) cans no-salt-added pinto beans (undrained)

1½ cups (360 ml) salsa

1½ teaspoons smoked paprika

1 teaspoon ground cumin

FOR TOPPING (OPTIONAL)

Diced avocado

Thinly sliced chives or scallions

Variations

- On less lazy days, cook your own beans from scratch! Simply use about 3 cups (720 g) total and ½ to 1 cup (120 to 240 ml) of the bean liquid or vegetable broth, to reach your desired consistency.

- To switch things up a bit, use black beans instead of pinto.

- Make it an Italian-inspired soup by using white beans and marinara sauce in place of the salsa, plus a generous handful of fresh or dried herbs (heavy on the basil and parsley).

1. To make the soup, add the beans, liquid and all, to a blender along with the salsa, paprika, and cumin. Blend until mostly smooth but with a bit of texture still remaining, as desired.

2. Transfer the mixture to a medium saucepan and heat over medium-high heat until steaming hot all the way through, 4 to 5 minutes. Alternatively, heat a single serving in the microwave for 2 minutes and store the rest in the fridge, sealed in an airtight container, for up to a week.

3. Ladle into bowls and top with the avocado and chives, if desired. Dig in!

MOROCCAN RED LENTIL STEW

Fragrant spices will perfume the entire kitchen when you get this highly aromatic stew bubbling on the stove. Thickened with red lentils and packed with protein, it's a hearty entrée to satisfy even the most monstrous appetites.

2 tablespoons (15 ml) olive oil

1 medium onion, diced

2 carrots, peeled and diced

1 tablespoon (8 g) ground ginger

1 tablespoon (8 g) smoked paprika

½ teaspoon ground turmeric

¼ teaspoon ground cinnamon

¼ teaspoon ground black pepper

1 pound (454 g) meatless ground beef, rehydrated TVP, or crumbled tempeh

1 cup (192 g) dried red lentils

1 (28-ounce [784 g]) can diced tomatoes

4 cups (960 ml) water

¼ cup (32 g) dried apricots, finely diced

2 tablespoons (30 ml) lemon juice

Salt and ground black pepper, to taste

1. Heat the oil in a large pot over medium heat. Once shimmering, add the onion and cook, stirring often, until translucent and lightly browned around the edges, 8 to 10 minutes.

2. Add the carrots, ginger, paprika, turmeric, cinnamon, and pepper, stir thoroughly to incorporate, and cook for 1 minute to begin releasing the essential oils.

3. Add the meatless beef and sauté, breaking up the grounds with your spatula, until browned, about 5 minutes.

4. Stir in the lentils and tomatoes, mixing well to incorporate, then add the water. Add the apricots, cover, and bring the mixture to a boil. Reduce the heat to keep the stew at a gentle simmer, and cook for 20 to 25 minutes, until the lentils are tender. Add the lemon juice and season with salt and pepper to taste.

5. If you'd like the soup to be creamier, let it sit for a few minutes and stir vigorously with a wide spatula to mash some of the lentils smooth.

6. The stew will continue to thicken as it cools, so you may want to adjust the amount of water if you have leftovers.

PURPLE RAINY DAY SOUP

Boldly magenta, or perhaps vividly violet, purple potatoes, black quinoa, and red cabbage join forces to create a stew of a different hue.

2 tablespoons (30 ml) olive oil

1 medium red onion, diced

4 cloves garlic, minced

4 cups (280 g) shredded red cabbage

⅓ cup (58 g) black quinoa

2 medium purple potatoes, peeled and diced (about 1 pound)

1 bay leaf

2 tablespoons (30 g) red miso paste

4 cups (960 ml) vegetable stock

½ teaspoon ground black pepper

½ teaspoon dried rosemary, crushed

1 tablespoon (15 ml) sherry vinegar

½ cup (75 g) frozen green peas

1. Heat the olive oil in a large stockpot over medium heat. Add the onion and sauté for about 5 minutes, until translucent. Add the garlic and continue cooking for another 5 to 10 minutes, until aromatic and lightly browned.

2. Add the shredded cabbage in handfuls, allowing it to wilt down slightly before adding more. Add the quinoa, potatoes, and bay leaf.

3. In a medium bowl, whisk the miso paste into the stock until smooth, then add it to the pot. Bring the mixture to a boil, reduce the heat, and cover. Simmer for 25 to 30 minutes, until the potatoes are fork-tender and the quinoa is fully cooked. Season with the black pepper, rosemary, and vinegar, adjusting to taste if needed.

4. Toss in the frozen peas and simmer just until thawed and hot all the way through. Serve right away while piping hot!

note

Naturally, if color is not your priority when it comes to dinner, you can use plain old green cabbage, white quinoa, or orange sweet potatoes. It will taste just as good in any hue!

SPANISH LENTIL SOUP

Keep warm and stay cozy with this simple, smoky lentil soup. Whole almonds make an unexpected appearance, slightly softened from the heat, still bearing a resounding crunch at the core. The unique combination of textures sets it apart from the pack.

2 tablespoons (30 ml) olive oil

1 medium yellow onion, diced

1 cup (110 g) diced celery

1 cup (120 g) shredded carrots

4 cloves garlic, minced

½ cup (120 g) tomato paste

1½ cups (290 g) black lentils

2½ teaspoons (7 g) smoked paprika

2 tablespoons (30 ml) apple cider vinegar

2 tablespoons (30 ml) soy sauce

½ cup (73 g) whole almonds

6 cups (1440 ml) water

Salt and ground black pepper, to taste

Finely minced fresh cilantro, for garnish (optional)

1. Heat the oil in a large stockpot over medium heat. Add the onion, celery, and carrots, and sauté until softened, 4 to 5 minutes.

2. Add the garlic and continue to cook, stirring periodically, for another 5 to 6 minutes, until the vegetables are lightly browned and highly aromatic.

3. Stir in the tomato paste, breaking it up as best you can. Add the lentils, paprika, vinegar, soy sauce, almonds, and water. Mix well to incorporate.

4. Cover and bring to a boil. Reduce the heat to medium-low and simmer for about 1 hour, until the lentils are tender.

5. Season with salt and pepper to taste. Ladle into bowls and top with fresh cilantro, if desired.

STRAWBERRY GAZPACHO

Balancing sweetness with savory undertones, the subtle bite of vinegar, and fresh verdant pop of basil, this unconventional chilled soup is a delicious study in contrasts.

4 cups (680 g) hulled and diced strawberries

1 medium cucumber, peeled and seeded if desired

1 red bell pepper, seeded and diced

1 (8-ounce [227 g]) can tomato sauce or puree

¼ cup (40 g) diced red onion

1 clove garlic

¼ cup (8 g) chopped fresh basil

1 teaspoon salt

½ teaspoon red pepper flakes

¼ cup (60 ml) sherry vinegar

¼ cup (60 ml) olive oil

Roughly chopped pistachios, additional sliced cucumbers, strawberries, and/or basil, for garnish (optional)

1. In a blender, combine the strawberries, cucumber, red pepper, tomato sauce, onion, garlic, basil, salt, red pepper flakes, and vinegar. Blend on high speed until thoroughly pureed.

2. With the motor running, slowly stream in the oil and puree until smooth and fully incorporated.

3. Transfer to the fridge and chill until ice cold, 1 to 3 hours.

4. Adjust the seasonings to taste, if needed. Ladle into bowls and garnish with the pistachios, cucumber, strawberries, and basil, if desired.

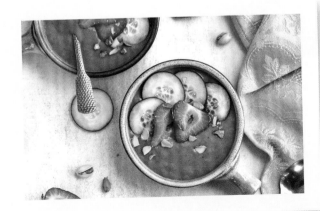

note

The gazpacho will keep in an airtight container in the fridge for 2 to 4 days.

TOM YAM NOODLE SOUP

Dropping the more typical addition of rice noodles in traditional tom yum soup in favor of spiralized yams, this sweet, sour, and spicy combination gains greater depth, and preparation is coincidentally simplified. Everything goes into one pot, cooks just to a boil, and dinner is served in an instant.

1 medium yam or sweet potato, peeled and spiralized

3 to 4 cups (720 to 960 ml) mushroom or vegetable stock

1 medium shallot, diced

1 inch (2.5 cm) fresh ginger, peeled and finely minced

1 medium Roma tomato, diced

6 to 8 ounces (168 to 227 g) medium-firm tofu, cubed

6 ounces (168 g) mixed mushrooms, sliced

2 tablespoons (30 ml) sriracha

2 teaspoons (10 ml) soy sauce

1½ tablespoons (23 ml) lime juice

¼ cup (4 g) minced fresh cilantro, for garnish (optional)

1. Add the spiralized yam to a large stockpot over medium heat. Pour in 3 cups (720 ml) of the stock to generously cover the vegetable noodles, adding more if needed, then add the shallot, ginger, tomato, tofu, mushrooms, sriracha, soy sauce, and lime juice.

2. Bring to a boil and simmer for about 10 minutes, until the yam noodles are fork-tender but well before they start falling apart.

3. Divide the soup between two big bowls, top with cilantro if desired, and dig in immediately, while piping hot!

Hearty Handheld Meals: Sandwiches, Tacos, Sliders, and More

chapter 7

CAULIFLOWER SLOPPY JOES

Simmering tender lentils and chopped cauliflower in a subtly sweet, rich tomato sauce makes this meatless marvel both boldly flavorful *and* brilliantly nutritious.

SLOPPY JOES

1 tablespoon (15 ml) olive oil

1 yellow onion, finely diced

1 red bell pepper, seeded and diced

2 cloves garlic, minced

1 pound (454 g) riced cauliflower

1½ cups (300 g) cooked brown or green lentils

1 (8-ounce [227 g]) can tomato sauce

1 cup (240 g) ketchup

2 tablespoons (30 g) tomato paste

1 tablespoon (15 ml) soy sauce

1 teaspoon smoked paprika

½ teaspoon salt

TO SERVE

4 hamburger buns

Sliced dill pickles

1. To make the Sloppy Joes, heat the oil in a medium skillet over medium heat. Add the onion, bell pepper, and garlic, and cook until soft and beginning to brown, stirring frequently, 4 to 5 minutes. Add the cauliflower and cook until tender, 4 to 5 minutes longer. Add the lentils, tomato sauce, ketchup, tomato paste, soy sauce, paprika, and salt, mixing to thoroughly combine.

2. Reduce the heat to medium-low and simmer gently, cooking until the sauce is slightly thickened and bubbling, 4 to 6 minutes.

3. To serve, divide the Sloppy Joe mixture among the hamburger buns and top each sandwich with pickles. Serve immediately, piping hot.

note

Leftovers can be stored in an airtight container in the fridge for 5 to 7 days.

CHEESESTEAK SANDWICHES

Soy curls soaked in umami-packed mushroom broth make up the "meat" of the matter here, tossed with lightly charred onions and roasted peppers, smothered under a blanket of gooey melted cheese. It's the kind of dish you could use to convert meat-lovers, cheese-lovers, and generally picky omnivores alike.

notes

If you can't find or don't like soy curls, feel free to use 1½ cups (200 g) of your favorite meatless beef strips instead. Just skip the soaking step and omit the broth.

Save some money and use the gooey cheese filling from page 141 [grilled cheese sandwiches] in place of the store-bought vegan provolone.

CHEESESTEAK FILLING

1½ cups (about 3 ounces [84 g]) dry soy curls

1½ cups (360 ml) mushroom broth, warmed

4 teaspoons (20 ml) olive oil

1 medium yellow onion, thinly sliced

1 red bell pepper, roasted, seeded, and thinly sliced

½ teaspoon dried oregano

¼ teaspoon freshly ground pepper

1 tablespoon (8 g) all-purpose flour

1 tablespoon (15 ml) reduced-sodium soy sauce

TO SERVE

3 hoagie rolls, split and toasted

9 slices provolone-style vegan cheese

1. To make the filling, place the dry soy curls in a large bowl and cover them with warmed mushroom broth. Let them soak for 15 to 20 minutes, until the soy curls are fully rehydrated and tender. Pour off but reserve any excess liquid.

2. Heat the oil in a large skillet over medium-high heat. Add the onion and sauté, stirring often, until browned around the edges, 4 to 5 minutes. Add the bell pepper, oregano, and ground pepper, and cook, stirring often, until the vegetables are wilted and soft, about 5 minutes. Reduce the heat to low, sprinkle the vegetables with the flour, and stir to coat.

3. Gently pour in ¼ cup (60 ml) of the reserved broth along with the soy sauce and bring the mixture up to a simmer. Cook for 2 minutes, then remove the pan from the heat.

4. To serve, divide the soy curl filling among the rolls and lay three provolone slices on top of each.

5. Place on a baking sheet and place under the broiler for 2 to 3 minutes, or heat in the microwave for 30 to 60 seconds, until the cheese is perfectly melted and gooey all over. Dig in immediately!

DELI-CIOUS EGGLESS SALAD SANDWICHES

No decent deli is complete without egg salad on the menu. No one said it had to be full of smelly hard-boiled eggs, though! Tofu makes for the perfect neutral base to lavish with seasonings, tangy pickles, and crunchy vegetables. Smear it on thick between two slices of bread, wrap it up, stuff it into pita, or just eat it with a fork; it's a staple that everyone should keep on hand.

TOFU EGG SALAD

1 pound (454 g) extra-firm tofu, drained and crumbled

1 cup (160 g) diced red onion

1 cup (130 g) finely diced dill pickles

1 cup (110 g) diced celery

3 tablespoons (18 g) nutritional yeast

1 tablespoon (7 g) onion powder

1 tablespoon (8 g) garlic powder

1 teaspoon ground black pepper

1 teaspoon ground turmeric

1 teaspoon salt

2 tablespoons (30 ml) apple cider vinegar

¾ cup (180 g) vegan mayonnaise

TO SERVE

8 slices sandwich bread

Baby greens, such as arugula, spinach, or spring mix

1. To make the tofu egg salad, in a large bowl, combine the crumbled tofu, onion, pickles, and celery.

2. In a small bowl, combine the nutritional yeast, onion powder, garlic powder, pepper, turmeric, and salt. Add the vinegar and mayonnaise, stirring gently to combine.

3. Add the creamy spice mixture to the tofu mixture and fold everything together to incorporate.

4. Store in an airtight container in the refrigerator for at least 1 hour before serving.

5. To serve, divide the tofu egg salad among four slices of bread, top with some baby greens, and place the remaining bread slices on top.

note

To reduce the fat and calories, use plain, unsweetened Greek-style vegan yogurt instead of mayonnaise.

PERFECT GRILLED CHEESE SANDWICHES

The very first thing I learned to "cook" for myself when I first went vegan was a grilled cheese sandwich. I say "cook" in quotation marks because it was more assembly than cooking, and barely even food-like, if we're being honest. Slap a waxy block of neon-orange vegan "cheez" between two slices of bread and stuff it into a panini press; walk away for 10 minutes and when you smell smoke, it's done! *Bon appétit!* Fortunately, the prepared vegan cheeses on the market have vastly improved since those dark ages, but there's still no need to resort to that quick fix when you can start from scratch for pennies on the dollar. This formula for luscious, gooey cheese sauce creates an ideal filling for grilled cheese sandwiches that would make your parents proud.

CHEESY FILLING

¼ cup (24 g) nutritional yeast

2 tablespoons (16 g) tapioca or potato starch

1 teaspoon apple cider vinegar

1 teaspoon salt

½ teaspoon onion powder

⅛ teaspoon hot paprika

⅛ teaspoon ground turmeric

1 cup (240 ml) plain nondairy milk

⅓ cup (80 g) tahini

TO SERVE

8 teaspoons (40 g) vegan butter or olive oil, divided

8 slices sandwich bread

1. To make the filling, whisk all the ingredients vigorously in a medium saucepan until completely smooth. If you have a blender, you can use it to make the process even easier. Set over medium-low heat and cook, whisking gently, for 5 to 7 minutes. The mixture should slowly thicken and seem slightly stretchy. Turn off the heat and set aside.

2. To assemble, spread 1 teaspoon of vegan butter over each slice of bread. Place two slices of bread in a medium skillet, buttered-sides down, over medium heat. Cook for 2 to 4 minutes, until the bottom is golden brown and evenly toasted. Smear about one-fourth of the cheese filling on one slice and cover with the second. Cook for just 1 to 2 minutes longer to heat all the way through.

3. Repeat with the remaining ingredients. Slice each sandwich in half and serve hot.

SWEET TEA PULLED JACKFRUIT SANDWICHES

Slowly simmered in an aromatic marinade inspired by sweet tea—an irreplaceable summertime brew designed for maximum refreshment—jackfruit tenderizes to a texture almost indistinguishable from pulled pork. Spiked with fresh lemon, it has a tart, sweet-and-sour balance, pulling out all the savory stops. Deceptively simple, the ginger-scallion slaw is not to be underestimated, nor overlooked. It is crisp and cooling, yet bright and invigorating in flavor, and I could honestly just eat it by the bowlful. It's an ideal foil to the richly meaty main and completes this deeply satisfying sandwich.

SWEET TEA PULLED JACKFRUIT

1 tablespoon (15 ml) olive oil

½ medium red onion, thinly sliced (about 1 cup)

2 cloves garlic, minced

1 teaspoon black tea leaves

3 tablespoons (36 g) granulated sugar

¼ cup (60 ml) lemon juice

¼ cup (60 ml) vegetable stock

2 tablespoons (30 ml) soy sauce

1 (14-ounce [392 g]) can young jackfruit, drained and rinsed

½ teaspoon dried rosemary, crushed

¼ teaspoon ground black pepper

GINGER-SCALLION SLAW

1 cup (100 g) roughly chopped scallion

1 inch (2.5 cm) fresh ginger, peeled and chopped

2 tablespoons (30 ml) lemon juice

2 tablespoons (30 ml) rice vinegar

¼ teaspoon salt

¼ cup (60 ml) olive oil

½ medium head green cabbage, shredded (about 6 cups)

1 cup (120 g) shredded carrots

TO SERVE

3 or 4 sandwich buns

1. To make the pulled jackfruit, heat the oil in a medium saucepan over medium heat. Add the onion and cook, stirring periodically, until softened and aromatic, 4 to 5 minutes. Add the garlic and tea leaves and cook until golden brown, 10 to 15 minutes. Stir in the sugar. Add the lemon juice, vegetable stock, and soy sauce all at once. Thoroughly scrape the bottom of the pan to make sure that nothing is sticking and burning.

2. Add the jackfruit, rosemary, and pepper, stirring gently to incorporate without splashing. Turn down the heat to medium-low and simmer until most of the liquid evaporates and the jackfruit is fork-tender, 20 to 30 minutes. Use the side of your spatula to roughly mash/shred the jackfruit.

3. To make the slaw, add the scallion, ginger, lemon juice, vinegar, and salt to a blender. Pulse to break down the more fibrous aromatics, pausing to scrape down the sides of the container if needed. With the motor running, slowly stream in the olive oil to achieve a creamy emulsification. Place the cabbage and carrots in a large bowl and pour the dressing over, mixing to thoroughly coat all the veggies.

4. To serve, lightly toast the buns and top with generous spoonfuls of the stewed jackfruit and slaw. Devour immediately! These are unapologetically messy sandwiches, so don't be afraid to dive right in without trying to be dainty about it. The buns will only grow progressively soggier once fully assembled.

TRIPLE CORN TOFU TACOS

Three cheers for corn in this triple-threat corn taco! The humble kernel is working overtime in this crowd-pleasing dish: soft corn tortillas are piled high with fresh corn kernels, crowned with crispy cornmeal-coated tofu. Crunchy cabbage and pico de gallo provide texture and flavor contrast. The tacos are then drizzled with a delicious avocado sauce, but unlike traditional crema, this one relies solely on the avocado for its creamy texture. Best of all, it's ready in 20 minutes from start to finish.

CORNMEAL-CRUSTED TOFU

½ cup (70 g) coarse yellow cornmeal

1 tablespoon (8 g) chili powder

1 teaspoon ground cumin

½ teaspoon salt

½ teaspoon garlic powder

¼ teaspoon ground black pepper

1 (14-ounce [392 g]) package extra-firm tofu, drained and cut into ¾-inch (2 cm) cubes

2 tablespoons (30 ml) olive oil

AVOCADO CREMA

1 ripe avocado, pitted and peeled

2 tablespoons (30 ml) lemon juice

1 tablespoon (15 ml) water, or more as needed

½ teaspoon ground cumin

¼ teaspoon salt

TO SERVE

8 corn tortillas, warmed

1 cup (70 g) shredded purple cabbage

1 cup (150 g) corn kernels

½ cup (120 g) fresh salsa or pico de gallo

1. To make the tofu, in a large bowl, add the cornmeal, chili powder, cumin, salt, garlic powder, and pepper. Stir to combine. Add the tofu and toss to coat.

2. Heat the oil in a large skillet over medium heat. Add about half the tofu so as not to crowd the pan. Let cook, undisturbed, to form a nice sear on the bottom, about 6 minutes. Gently flip and continue to sauté until golden and crispy on all sides, about 5 minutes more; transfer to a plate and repeat with the remaining tofu.

3. To make the crema, add the avocado, lemon juice, water, cumin, and salt to a blender and puree, pausing to scrape down the sides as needed, until completely smooth. Slowly drizzle in more water until it reaches your desired consistency. Add more water if using the crema as a sauce, less if using it as a spread. Alternatively, put the ingredients into a deep bowl or pot and blend with an immersion blender until smooth.

4. To serve, top each tortilla with equal portions of the cabbage, corn, and salsa. Add 3 or 4 cubes of the tofu, then slather with the avocado crema.

CRISPY CAULIFLOWER TACOS

Spicy pan-seared cauliflower takes center stage on soft corn tortillas, wrapped up with crisp greens, creamy avocado, and a hearty spread of refried beans. Though simple in concept, the contrasting flavors and textures dazzle when combined. Depart from tradition to enjoy a bold new approach to preparing those unassuming white florets.

1 tablespoon (15 ml) olive oil

1 clove garlic, minced

½ medium head cauliflower, cut into florets (about 2 heaping cups)

½ small red onion, thinly sliced

½ teaspoon hot paprika

¼ teaspoon cayenne pepper

¼ teaspoon salt

1 tablespoon (15 ml) lime juice

4 (6-inch [15 cm]) corn tortillas, warmed

1 cup (240 g) refried beans, warmed

1 cup (70 g) shredded green cabbage or romaine lettuce

¼ cup (4 g) minced fresh cilantro

1 small avocado, peeled, pitted, and sliced

1. Heat the olive oil in a medium pan over medium heat. Add the garlic and cauliflower, and cook for about 5 minutes, until the vegetables just begin to brown. Add the onion and continue to sauté for 15 minutes, stirring occasionally, to caramelize the onions and sear the cauliflower all over.

2. Mix in the paprika, cayenne according to your heat preference, salt, and lime juice. Cook for just 2 more minutes to toast the spices.

3. Spread each tortilla with a spoonful of the beans. Top with equal portions of the cabbage, cilantro, and avocado. Divide the cauliflower mixture among the tortillas and serve immediately.

taco Tuesday

THAI COCONUT SLIDERS

Taking inspiration from their Asian origins, Thai spices join the mix to form tender patties, fashioned into bite-size sliders perfect for celebrating the tail end of summer. They aren't beefy burgers by any stretch of the imagination, and they don't try to be. Instead, they celebrate the coconut in all its natural glory, succulent and tender, cradled between two buns. Mock meats need not apply.

THAI-SPICED COCONUT PATTIES

2 tablespoons (30 ml) olive oil, divided

½ cup (80 g) diced shallot

2 cloves garlic, minced

2 tablespoons (30 g) red curry paste

1 tablespoon (15 g) ketchup

1 tablespoon (15 ml) soy sauce

1 tablespoon (15 ml) lime juice

1 cup (80 g) dry coconut pulp or meal

1 cup (200 g) cooked jasmine rice

2 tablespoons (16 g) tapioca flour

Salt and ground black pepper, to taste

TO SERVE

7 or 8 mini slider buns

Sliced cucumbers

Sliced avocado

Fresh cilantro or Thai basil

ADDITIONAL TOPPING SUGGESTIONS

Peanut sauce

Mango relish or chutney

Coconut aioli

1. To make the patties, heat 1 tablespoon (15 ml) of the oil in a medium pan over medium heat. Add the shallot and garlic, and sauté until softened and aromatic, 3 to 4 minutes. Stir in the curry paste and cook for 2 to 3 minutes to bring out the full flavors of the spices. Add the ketchup, soy sauce, and lime juice, and cook for another 3 minutes, allowing the ingredients to meld.

2. Transfer the aromatics to a large bowl along with the coconut pulp, cooked rice, and tapioca flour. Use a wide spatula to mix everything together. It's a very thick mixture so you may just want to get in there with your hands to speed up the process. Add salt and pepper to taste.

3. Use an ice cream scoop to portion out 7 or 8 sliders, or just aim for a scant ¼ cup (60 g) per patty. Roll them between lightly moistened hands and press them down gently to shape.

4. Heat the remaining 1 tablespoon (15 ml) oil in a wide skillet over medium heat. Cook 2 or 3 sliders at a time, being careful not to crowd the pan, for 5 to 8 minutes per side, until golden brown, flipping as needed.

5. To serve, place the patties on mini slider buns with as many toppings as your heart desires.

notes

Let the cooked patties cool completely and freeze in an airtight container for up to 6 months.

Oat flour can be used instead of protein powder for a high-fiber alternative.

PUMPKIN POWER BURGERS

Burgers are one of the most reliable staples to be found in any cook's arsenal. They are infinitely adjustable, easily prepared, and universally enjoyed, and many satisfying meals both past and present can be attributed to the humble patty. Pumpkin puree is the secret ingredient holding these particular patties together in this crowd-pleasing, protein-packed formula.

PUMPKIN PATTIES

2 tablespoons (30 ml) olive oil, divided

2 cloves garlic, minced

1 cup (160 g) diced onion

1 teaspoon balsamic vinegar

1 (14-ounce [392 g]) can (1¾ cups [360 g] cooked) chickpeas, drained

½ cup (120 g) pumpkin puree

1 tablespoon (11 g) yellow mustard

1 teaspoon ground cumin

¼ teaspoon dried oregano

½ cup (60 g) plain, unsweetened vegan protein powder

Salt and ground black pepper

TO SERVE

Mustard

6 to 8 burger buns

Sliced tomatoes

Arugula

1. To make the patties, heat 1 tablespoon (15 ml) of the olive oil in a medium skillet over medium heat. When shimmering, add the garlic and onion, and sauté until aromatic and lightly golden brown, 6 to 8 minutes. Add the balsamic vinegar, scrape the bottom of the pan to get up all the brown bits, turn off the heat, and let cool for about 10 minutes.

2. In a separate bowl, roughly mash the beans with a fork or potato masher. You want to keep the texture fairly coarse so that the burger maintains a satisfying bite. Add the pumpkin puree, mustard, cumin, oregano, and protein powder, mixing well to incorporate. Add the sautéed vegetables and mix thoroughly, making sure that there are no pockets of dry ingredients remaining. The mixture should be soft but manageable, something you can easily mold into patties that will hold their shape. Season with salt and pepper to taste.

3. Measure out between ⅓ to ½ cup (80 to 120 g) of the burger mixture for each patty, and form them into round, flat pucks with slightly moistened hands. You should get 6 to 8 burgers.

4. Clean and dry the skillet before returning it to the stove over medium heat. Heat the remaining 1 tablespoon (15 ml) oil and cook the patties, 3 at a time, being careful not to crowd the pan. Sear on the first side by letting them cook, undisturbed, for 10 to 15 minutes, until evenly golden all over. Flip and cook for 10 minutes longer, until equally brown. Remove from the pan and repeat with the remaining patties.

5. To serve, spread mustard on the bottom buns and top with layers of sliced tomatoes, the patties, and a few arugula leaves, then finish with the top bun.

ISRAELI PITA PIZZAS

Pita bread is best known for its spacious pockets, but left whole and baked in the oven, the Middle Eastern flatbread can also become a crispy personal pizza crust. Dressed up with a thick smear of hummus, a bright palate of fresh vegetables, and a lemon tahini drizzle, it's a definite departure from the usual red sauce option, and in the best way possible. You'll never miss the cheese or marinara with this quick and easy combination.

LEMON TAHINI DRIZZLE

3 tablespoons (45 g) tahini

3 tablespoons (45 g) plain, unsweetened vegan yogurt

1 to 2 tablespoons (15 to 30 ml) lemon juice

PITA PIZZAS

2 medium pita breads

2 teaspoons (10 ml) olive oil

1 clove garlic, finely minced

⅔ cup (160 g) prepared hummus

1 cup (150 g) cherry or grape tomatoes, halved

¼ cup (25 g) sliced olives

¼ cup (16 g) roughly chopped fresh parsley

1 scallion, thinly sliced

1. To make the tahini drizzle, whisk together all the ingredients in a small bowl until smooth, adjusting the lemon juice to taste.

2. To make the pizzas, heat a large skillet over medium heat. Brush the pita breads with the olive oil and sprinkle the minced garlic evenly on top. Place in the hot skillet and cook for 4 to 6 minutes, until lightly toasted.

3. Divide the hummus between the two pitas, covering them generously but leaving the perimeter clear. Top with the tomatoes, olives, parsley, and scallions. Drizzle with the lemon tahini sauce and serve immediately.

MUJADDARA ONIGIRI

Ordinarily, the only thing that mujaddara and onigiri have in common is rice. The former is a spiced pilaf with tender lentils and sweet caramelized onions, while the latter is a triangle of sticky sushi rice wrapped in nori. When the two concepts collide, however, it tastes like it was meant to be.

1 cup (240 ml) water

¾ cup (150 g) sushi rice

1½ tablespoons (23 ml) olive oil

12 ounces (340 g) onions, chopped (about 2 cups [320 g])

¼ to ½ teaspoon salt, divided

¼ teaspoon ground cumin

1½ teaspoons balsamic vinegar

⅛ teaspoon ground cinnamon

¼ teaspoon freshly ground black pepper

3 tablespoons (12 g) chopped fresh parsley

1 cup (200 g) cooked brown lentils

1. Bring the water to a boil in a medium saucepan over medium heat. Once at a lively bubble, stir in the sushi rice and immediately reduce the heat all the way to low. Cover and cook gently for 15 to 20 minutes, until the water has been fully absorbed. Turn off the heat and let stand, covered, for an additional 10 minutes.

2. Meanwhile, heat the oil in a medium skillet with high sides over medium heat. When hot and shimmering, add the onions and turn the heat down to medium-low. Cook for 10 minutes, stirring occasionally, until translucent. When they begin to brown around the edges, add ¼ teaspoon of the salt and reduce the heat further. Continue to cook over low heat, stirring every now and then, for about an additional 30 minutes to caramelize the onions. Be sure to scrape the bottom of the pan thoroughly to prevent pieces from sticking and burning. The onions should take on a deep amber-brown color and be very aromatic. Remove the pan from the heat, stir in the cumin, balsamic vinegar, cinnamon, and pepper, and let cool.

3. When both the rice and the onions are cool enough to handle, just above room temperature, mix them together in a large bowl along with the parsley and lentils. Stir well to thoroughly distribute all the ingredients. Add the remaining ¼ teaspoon of salt, to taste.

4. Scoop out approximately ⅓ to ½ cup (80 to 120 g) of the mixture for each onigiri, gently pressing it into triangles in the palms of your hands. If the rice isn't quite holding together properly, let it sit and continue to cool for a bit longer. Serve immediately or wrap each individually in plastic to save for later. Stored in the fridge, the prepared onigiri will keep for up to 3 days.

LETTUCE
CILANTRO
BELL PEPPERS
TOMATOES
AVOCADOS
CORN ON THE COB
VEGETABLE STOCK
YELLOW CORNMEAL

Bowl-in-One

chapter 8

EASY GREEN CURRY

You can have a fiery bowlful of green curry using this recipe, and the results will be far healthier and fresher than takeout. With curry paste and coconut milk stocked in your pantry, this easy meal is never more than a few minutes away.

1 tablespoon (15 ml) olive oil

1 pound (454 g) extra-firm tofu, thoroughly drained and cubed

1 tablespoon (15 ml) soy sauce

2 tablespoons (30 g) green curry paste

2 (14-ounce [392 g]) cans full-fat coconut milk

2 small sweet potatoes, peeled and diced

3 cups (210 g) broccoli florets

½ cup (8 g) minced fresh cilantro

2 tablespoons (30 ml) lime juice

1 avocado, sliced

1. Heat the oil in a stockpot over medium-high heat. Add the tofu and soy sauce, and cook, stirring gently to coat the pieces without breaking them, until golden brown, 10 to 12 minutes; remove with a slotted spoon to a bowl.

2. Stir the curry paste and coconut milk together in the stockpot; add the sweet potatoes and bring to a boil. Reduce the heat to medium-low and cook the potatoes at a simmer until fork-tender, about 10 minutes.

3. Add the broccoli and tofu to the sweet potatoes and cook until the broccoli is bright green, about 5 minutes more.

4. Remove the pot from heat. Add the cilantro and lime juice and stir to combine. Spoon into bowls and top with the avocado.

note

Any variety of vegetables will fit the bill; don't be afraid to experiment with anything you find sitting in the fridge, begging to be eaten! If you have extra time, press the tofu cubes between a pair of baking sheets lined with paper towel to remove excess moisture. The drier your tofu, the better the end results.

SRI LANKAN–STYLE CASHEW CURRY

This is a dish that I often whip up for myself for a quick dinner; it's easy to eat, and admittedly, almost embarrassing to spill the details about. You know those meals that you love but would never serve to anyone else? That is this curry. Although it was undeniably inspired by Sri Lankan curry, featuring cashews soaked for hours to lend them a uniquely creamy yet toothsome texture, my take is entirely inauthentic, but is everything I crave on a busy weeknight. If you'd prefer crunchier cashews, skip the soaking and toss them in at the very end.

1½ cups (210 g) whole, raw cashews, optionally soaked in water to cover for 2 hours

1 tablespoon (15 ml) olive oil or coconut oil

1 large yellow onion, diced

3 to 4 cloves garlic, minced

1 inch (2.5 cm) fresh ginger, peeled and minced

½ cup (120 ml) vegetable stock or water

2 to 3 tablespoons (16 to 24 g) yellow curry powder

1 large sweet potato or 2 medium, peeled and chopped

2 medium zucchini, halved lengthwise and chopped

1 (14-ounce [392 g]) can light coconut milk

1 tablespoon (15 ml) soy sauce

2 cups (300 g) frozen peas

Salt and ground black pepper, to taste

1. Rinse and thoroughly drain your cashews if soaking; set aside.

2. Heat the oil in a large pot over medium heat. Add the onion and cook, stir occasionally to prevent sticking and burning, until soften and translucent, about 5 minutes. Add the garlic and ginger, and sauté for 8 to 10 minutes longer, so that everything is very lightly caramelized and highly aromatic. Add the vegetable stock and scrape up any tasty brown bits that may be clinging to the bottom of the pot.

3. Add the cashews, curry powder, sweet potatoes, zucchini, coconut milk, and soy sauce. Stir well to incorporate, cover, and simmer for about 15 minutes, until the sweet potatoes are fork-tender. Turn off the heat and add the peas straight out of the freezer. No need to thaw, as they'll immediately come up to temperature once they hit the hot curry. Add salt and pepper to taste and serve hot.

 note
For a lower-fat (and lower-cost) alternative, swap the cashews for 2 to 3 cups (480 to 720 g) cooked white kidney beans.

"BEEFY" RICE

Here's another simple one-pot wonder that may be ugly to look at but is truly comforting to eat. This one-pot prep means that cleanup is a breeze, too.

2 tablespoons (30 ml) olive oil

1 large red onion, diced

3 cloves garlic, minced

6 ounces (168 g) cremini, portobello, or button mushrooms, roughly chopped

12 ounces (340 g) meatless grounds or crumbled tempeh

2 tablespoons (12 g) nutritional yeast

1 tablespoon (2 g) dried parsley

1½ teaspoons Italian seasoning

1½ cups (300 g) uncooked white long-grain rice

4 cups (960 ml) vegetable stock

Salt and ground black pepper, to taste

1. Heat the oil in a medium pot over medium-high heat. Once shimmering, add the onion and garlic, and cook until softened, aromatic, and beginning to brown around the edges, 6 to 8 minutes.

2. Add the mushrooms and meatless grounds, using your spatula to break up the meat. Sauté until the mushrooms soften and the meat is no longer pink, 5 to 6 minutes.

3. Lower the heat to medium, add the nutritional yeast, parsley, Italian seasoning, and rice, stir to combine, and cook for 2 minutes.

4. Slowly pour in the vegetable stock, stirring once more to combine. Cover, bring to a simmer, and reduce the heat to low.

5. Cook gently for 14 to 18 minutes, until the liquid is almost entirely absorbed. Turn off the heat but keep covered. Let rest for 5 minutes to finish steaming.

6. Season with salt and pepper to taste.

note

This would be great with a dollop of vegan sour cream on top.

MANGO CHILI

Dig into a big bowl of black bean chili with the tropical sweetness of mango. It's a warming, stick-to-your-ribs kind of dish that won't weigh you down.

1½ tablespoons (23 ml) olive oil

1 small yellow onion, diced

1 red bell pepper, seeded and diced

3 cloves garlic, minced

1 tablespoon (8 g) chili powder

1 teaspoon dried oregano

¾ teaspoon ground cumin

¼ teaspoon cayenne pepper

1 (14-ounce [392 g]) can black beans, drained and rinsed

1 (14-ounce [392 g]) can diced tomatoes

1 medium mango, peeled, pitted, and diced

¼ cup (4 g) chopped fresh cilantro

1 avocado, peeled, pitted, and sliced

1. Heat the oil in a large saucepan over medium-high heat. Add the onion, bell pepper, and garlic, and cook until the onions are translucent and the vegetables have softened, 6 to 8 minutes.

2. Add the chili powder, oregano, cumin, and cayenne and stir to combine. Sauté for just 1 minute, until aromatic. Add the black beans, diced tomatoes, and mango. Stir to combine, bring to a boil, and immediately reduce the heat to medium-low. Simmer gently for 15 to 20 minutes, stirring occasionally, for the flavors to meld and the chili to thicken.

3. Ladle into bowls and top with the fresh cilantro and avocado slices.

4. Leftover chili will keep for up to 1 week in the refrigerator or frozen in individual servings for up to 2 months.

FIDEO RISOTTO

Referred to by some as "Mexican spaghetti," fideo is the simple sort of pasta dish that has nearly universal appeal thanks to both its flavor and its ease of preparation. Typically served dry as a side dish or flooded with broth as a soup, this dish falls somewhere in between—a thick stew of vegetables and pasta that could be eaten either with a spoon or a fork, depending on how long the noodles are cooked.

Silky strands of broken spaghetti boast a uniquely nutty taste thanks to a quick sauté before cooking, setting this dish apart from your average heap of pale pasta. Roasted peppers mingle among the short strands, harmonizing with the essences of smoked paprika and cumin to render a wholly warming, revitalizing bowl full of edible comfort.

3 tablespoons (45 ml) olive oil, divided

8 ounces (227 g) broken or cut spaghetti

½ large red onion, diced

3 cloves garlic, minced

2 Roma tomatoes, diced

1 roasted poblano pepper, seeded and diced

1 roasted red pepper, seeded and diced

3 cups (720 ml) low-sodium vegetable broth

3 tablespoons (45 ml) lime juice

2 tablespoons (12 g) nutritional yeast

1½ teaspoons smoked paprika

1½ teaspoons ground cumin

1 cup (150 g) corn kernels, canned and drained or frozen and thawed

½ cup (8 g) chopped fresh cilantro

Salt and ground black pepper, to taste

¼ cup (38 g) toasted pepitas (optional)

1. Heat 1½ tablespoons (23 ml) of the oil in a large stockpot over medium heat. Once shimmering, add the pasta and stir to coat. Sauté the noodles, stirring frequently, until toasted and golden brown all over, 5 to 8 minutes. Remove the noodles from the pot and set aside.

2. Heat the remaining 1½ tablespoons (23 ml) oil in the pot over medium heat. Add the onion and garlic, and cook until softened and aromatic, 4 to 5 minutes. Add the tomatoes and both roasted peppers, and cook, stirring periodically, until the onions are lightly golden, 4 to 5 minutes.

3. Add the vegetable broth, lime juice, nutritional yeast, paprika, and cumin. Bring the liquid to a boil, then return the toasted noodles to the pot. Stir well to incorporate, cover, and reduce the heat to medium-low. Simmer gently until the pasta is tender and the liquid mostly absorbed, 9 to 11 minutes.

4. Add the corn and cilantro, then remove from the heat. Season with salt and pepper to taste. Ladle into bowls and top individual servings with a tablespoon or so of pepitas, if desired.

HOPPIN' JOHN RISOTTO

Hoppin' John, the Southern staple featuring collard greens, black-eyed peas, and rice, has tons of unfulfilled potential. It's typically weighed down with pork but light on spices, so there's ample room for improvement. Turning the dish into a creamy, well-balanced risotto, it can play the role of either a side or the star of the show on any dinner table. Incredibly savory and soothing, it's the perfect heart-warming and rib-sticking dish on colder days. Be sure to prep all the vegetables so that it's a streamlined process to add them when needed.

note

Purists may cry foul, but yes, sushi rice is my grain of choice for risotto. Arborio or carnaroli are the "correct" options, but I find sushi rice every bit as creamy, tender, and clean-tasting, not to mention far cheaper.

4½ to 5 cups (1080 to 1200 ml) vegetable stock

2 tablespoons (30 ml) olive oil

1 medium yellow onion, diced

½ medium red, orange, or yellow bell pepper, seeded and diced

2 stalks celery, diced

3 to 4 cloves garlic, finely minced

1½ cups (300 g) sushi rice

½ cup (120 ml) water

½ cup (120 ml) full-fat coconut milk

2 tablespoons (30 ml) soy sauce

¼ cup (24 g) nutritional yeast

1½ teaspoons dried thyme

½ teaspoon dried oregano

1 dried bay leaf

¼ teaspoon red pepper flakes

¼ teaspoon freshly ground black pepper, plus more to taste

½ teaspoon liquid smoke

1 (14-ounce [392 g]) can black-eyed peas, drained and rinsed

1 bunch (about 1 pound [454 g]) fresh collard greens, thoroughly washed and dried, stemmed and chopped

Salt, to taste

1. Pour the vegetable stock into a saucepan and heat over medium heat. Keep this covered, just below a simmer at all times.

2. Heat the oil in a large saucepan over medium heat. Add the onion and sauté for 2 to 4 minutes, until semitransparent and aromatic. Add the bell pepper, celery, and garlic, and cook, stirring occasionally, for 5 to 8 minutes, until the vegetables are just barely beginning to brown around the edges. Add the rice, stirring well to coat with the oil and vegetable liquid, and cook for about 2 minutes or until somewhat translucent in appearance.

3. Slowly pour in the water, carefully scraping up any bits that might be stuck to the bottom. Turn down the heat to medium-low. Add the coconut milk, soy sauce, nutritional yeast, thyme, oregano, bay leaf, red pepper flakes, black pepper, and liquid smoke. Bring the liquid up to a simmer, and once it has mostly absorbed into the rice, add 1 cup (240 ml) of the hot stock. Continue to cook gently, stirring every few minutes to check on the consistency, adding in another ½ to 1 cup (120 to 240 ml) of the stock as needed. The rice should cook for about 20 to 25 minutes, until tender but creamy. Always keep the mixture looking somewhat saucy without being soupy; remember, this is not a pilaf where you want dry, distinct grains.

4. In the final 10 minutes of cooking, add the beans and greens, adding the greens a few handfuls at a time so that they can wilt down and not overflow out of the pot.

5. Add salt and pepper to taste and remove the bay leaf before serving. Enjoy immediately, as the rice will continue to thicken as it cools.

SHOR NAKHOD

How do you turn a giant bowl of potatoes into a semirespectable complete meal? Just add beans! Modeled after the classic Afghan dish, chickpeas meet tender potatoes in a simple, tangy, herbaceous dressing. Cilantro is the main feature here, so haters should steer clear. Sorry, genetically misfortunate friends.

8 ounces (227 g) Yukon gold potatoes, diced

1 (14-ounce [392 g]) can chickpeas, drained and rinsed

¼ cup (25 g) roughly chopped scallion

½ cup (8 g) roughly chopped cilantro

¼ cup (60 ml) rice vinegar

¼ teaspoon salt

⅛ teaspoon ground black pepper

1. Place the potatoes in a medium saucepan and cover with water. Set over medium heat, bring to a boil, and cook until fork-tender. Drain and rinse with cold water to immediately stop the cooking process. Transfer to a large bowl and add the chickpeas.

2. Meanwhile, combine the scallion, cilantro, vinegar, salt, and pepper in a food processor. Pulse until it looks like pesto: slightly coarse, but well blended. Alternatively, you can mince the mixture by hand very finely for a low-tech, "rustic" approach.

3. Add the pesto to the potatoes and chickpeas and toss to thoroughly coat. For the best flavor, chill for at least an hour before serving.

note

Shor Nakhod will keep beautifully in the fridge for up to a week.

GREEK SPAGHETTI SQUASH BOAT

Want a big, fat Greek bowlful of pasta, but not the carb coma that inevitably follows? Replace those starchy strands with spaghetti squash and instantly boost your vegetable intake with ease. Serve it right out of the squash shells for a fun bowl-in-one presentation.

1 medium (about 2½-pound [1135 g]) spaghetti squash

2 tablespoons (30 ml) olive oil

½ small red onion, diced

2 cloves garlic, minced

1 medium red bell pepper, seeded and diced

1 (5-ounce [140 g]) package fresh baby spinach

1 (6-ounce [168 g]) jar marinated artichokes, drained and roughly chopped

8 ounces (227 g, or ½ package) extra-firm tofu, drained and crumbled

¼ cup (25 g) sliced black olives

2 tablespoons (30 ml) red wine vinegar

2 tablespoons (4 g) minced fresh basil

1 teaspoon Dijon mustard

¾ teaspoon dried oregano

½ teaspoon ground black pepper

1. Pierce the spaghetti squash with a fork in a straight line down the center. Place in a microwave-safe dish and microwave for 5 minutes. Let stand until cool enough to handle. Slice the squash in half lengthwise, down the line of fork pricks, and use a sturdy spoon to scoop out the stringy seeds; compost or discard.

2. Pour ¼ cup (60 ml) water into the microwave-safe dish. Return the squash halves to the dish, cut-side down. Microwave for another 8 to 10 minutes, or until fork-tender. Let sit until cool enough to handle.

3. Meanwhile, heat the oil in a medium skillet over medium heat. Add the onion, garlic, and bell pepper, and sauté until golden brown, 10 to 15 minutes.

4. Add the spinach a few handfuls at a time, stirring until it wilts down to a more manageable volume. Fold in the artichokes, tofu, olives, vinegar, basil, mustard, oregano, and pepper, and cook for just a few minutes longer to warm the mixture through.

5. When the spaghetti squash is cool enough to handle, scrape a fork back and forth across the flesh to remove thread-like strands, keeping a border around the outsides to ensure that the shells remain intact.

6. Mix the "spaghetti" strands into the filling, stirring until well distributed throughout. Distribute the filling equally between the two halves, piling it up high, and serve immediately.

SMOKY TOFU AND VEGETABLE MULTIGRAIN BOWL

More than a mere rice bowl, this bountiful dish features tender mixed grains topped with tofu and an array of vegetables. A sultry, smoky sauce brings the perfect finish.

MULTIGRAIN BASE

3 cups (720 ml) vegetable stock

1 cup (165 g) brown rice

⅔ cup (115 g) quinoa

⅓ cup (53 g) wild rice

SMOKY HOISIN SAUCE

½ cup (120 g) hoisin sauce

3 tablespoons (45 ml) water, or more to taste

1 tablespoon (15 ml) rice vinegar

½ teaspoon liquid smoke

½ teaspoon ground ginger

½ teaspoon garlic powder

TO ASSEMBLE

1 (8-ounce [227 g]) package smoked or baked tofu, sliced

1½ cups (180 g) shredded carrots

3 Persian cucumbers or 1 seedless English cucumber, thinly sliced

1 Chioggia or red beet, peeled and thinly sliced

2 avocados, peeled, pitted, and sliced

¼ cup (36 g) toasted sesame seeds

½ cup (15 g) daikon radish sprouts

1. To make the multigrain base, combine the vegetable stock, brown rice, quinoa, and wild rice in a saucepan; bring to a boil over medium-high heat. Place a lid on the saucepan, reduce the heat to low, and simmer until the liquid has been fully absorbed, 35 to 45 minutes. Remove from the heat but leave the pot covered to keep warm.

2. To make the sauce, combine the hoisin sauce, water, rice vinegar, liquid smoke, ginger, and garlic powder in a bowl. Stir to blend and thin with more water if needed.

3. To assemble the bowls, divide the multigrain base among four large bowls; top with the tofu, carrot, cucumber, beet, avocado, sesame seeds, and sprouts. Drizzle the smoky hoisin sauce on top.

SOUTHWESTERN SWEET POTATO SPIRAL BOWL

Scrounging through the fridge for a more reasonable dinner than greasy takeout or cold cereal, I never intended to make something photo-worthy, but the results were too beautiful to ignore. Spinning up an orange-fleshed spud instead of squash started out my bowl with a hearty, substantial base for a Southwestern-inspired celebration of summer.

QUICK CHIPOTLE CREMA

¾ cup (105 g) raw cashews

½ cup (120 ml) water

2 tablespoons (30 ml) lime juice

1 canned chipotle chile in adobo plus 2 tablespoons (30 ml) adobo sauce

1 tablespoon (15 g) tomato paste

2 teaspoons (4 g) nutritional yeast

½ teaspoon salt

TO ASSEMBLE

8 ounces (227 g) spiralized sweet potato, raw or lightly steamed

⅓ cup (50 g) corn kernels

½ cup (120 g) chickpeas

½ avocado, sliced

⅓ cup (50 g) cherry tomatoes, halved

¼ cup (60 g) salsa

½ cup (15 g) shredded lettuce

⅓ cup (40 g) sliced bell pepper

1. To make the crema, combine all the ingredients in a blender and crank it up to high. Thoroughly puree until completely smooth, pausing to scrape down the sides of the container if needed. You will likely have much more crema than needed for one portion, but trust me, you'll wish there was even more left over once you taste this stuff. In fact, feel free to double the quantities and save the sauce in an airtight container in the fridge for up to a week.

2. To assemble, spoon a generous dollop or two of the chipotle crema onto the spiralized sweet potato and toss to thoroughly coat the noodles. Place in a large bowl and pile the corn, chickpeas, avocado, tomatoes, salsa, lettuce, and bell pepper on top in an attractive pattern, or just toss it all together. Dig in!

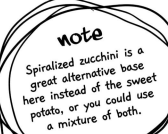

note

Spiralized zucchini is a great alternative base here instead of the sweet potato, or you could use a mixture of both.

TACO-STUFFED SWEET POTATOES

Tortillas need not apply when you can pile tender sweet potatoes high with all your favorite taco night toppers instead! Southwestern-spiced black beans make this meatless main a hearty and delicious alternative to the usual routine.

4 medium sweet potatoes	1 teaspoon ground cumin
1 tablespoon (15 ml) olive oil	1 teaspoon smoked paprika
1 medium red bell pepper, seeded and diced	1 teaspoon chili powder
2 cloves garlic, minced	1 tablespoon (15 ml) lime juice
1 cup (150 g) frozen corn kernels, thawed	½ cup (60 g) shredded vegan cheese
1 (14-ounce [392 g]) can black beans, drained and rinsed	1 tomato, diced
	2 scallions, thinly sliced
1 tablespoon (15 g) tomato paste	½ cup (8 g) roughly chopped fresh cilantro

note

If you're craving more traditional tacos, feel free to dice the potatoes before cooking and pile everything into corn tortillas to serve.

1. Wash the sweet potatoes thoroughly, pat dry, and pierce a few times with a fork. Place on a microwave-safe plate and microwave for 4 to 5 minutes. If the potatoes aren't fork-tender after 5 minutes, continue microwaving in 1-minute increments. Let cool for a few minutes until you can handle them without burning your hands.

2. Meanwhile, heat the oil in a medium skillet over medium heat. Add the red pepper and garlic, and sauté until the vegetables are soft and aromatic. Mix in the corn, beans, tomato paste, cumin, paprika, chili powder, and lime juice. Stir thoroughly and cook for 15 minutes to allow the flavors to meld.

3. Split each baked sweet potato in half and scrape out some of the flesh, leaving a sturdy border intact to support the outer skin. Add this to the bean mixture, stir well to incorporate, and then distribute equally among the potatoes, mounding it up high. Sprinkle evenly with the vegan cheese and return the potatoes to the microwave for just 30 to 60 seconds to melt the cheese.

4. Top with the diced tomatoes, scallions, and cilantro. Serve right away, while piping hot!

ABOUT THE AUTHOR

Hannah Kaminsky is the creator, writer, and photographer behind the award-winning vegan blog *Bittersweet* (bittersweetblog.com). She contributes regularly to VegNews and Allergic Living, and she has created recipes for VitaSoy, So Delicious, and other leading brands. She has also written *Sweet Vegan Treats*, *Vegan Desserts*, and *Real Food, Real Fast*. She lives and works in Austin, Texas.

INDEX